D1518619

INSIDE THE TRANSPUTER

COMPUTER SCIENCE TEXTS

COMPUTER SCIENCE TEXTS

Inside the Transputer

DAVID A. P. MITCHELL

BSc
Researcher, Department of Computer Science
Sheffield University

JONATHAN A. THOMPSON

BSc, MPhil
Senior Experimental Officer, Department of Computer Science
Sheffield University

GORDON A. MANSON

BSc, PhD, MSc
Lecturer, Department of Computer Science
Sheffield University

GRAHAM R. BROOKES

MA, PhD, MSc
Professor of Computer Science, Department of Computer Science
Hull University

BLACKWELL SCIENTIFIC PUBLICATIONS

OXFORD LONDON EDINBURGH
BOSTON MELBOURNE

© D. A. Mitchell, J. A. Thompson,
G. A. Manson, G. R. Brookes, 1990

Blackwell Scientific Publications
Editorial offices:
Osney Mead, Oxford OX2 0EL
25 John Street, London WC1N 2EU
23 Ainslie Place, Edinburgh EH3 6AJ
3 Cambridge Center, Suite 208
  Cambridge, Massachusetts 02142, USA
107 Barry Street, Carlton
  Victoria 3053, Australia

First published 1990

Printed and bound in Great Britain by
Mackays of Chatham PLC, Chatham, Kent

DISTRIBUTORS

Marston Book Services Ltd
PO Box 87
Oxford OX2 0DT
(Orders: Tel: 0865 791155
        Fax: 0865 791927
        Telex: 837515

USA
  Publishers' Business Services
  PO Box 447
  Brookline Village
  Massachusetts 02147
  (Orders: Tel (617) 524–7678)

Canada
  Oxford University Press
  70 Wynford Drive
  Don Mills
  Ontario M3C 1J9
  (Orders: Tel (416) 441–2941)

Australia
  Blackwell Scientific Publications
  (Australia) Pty Ltd
  107 Barry Street
  Carlton, Victoria 3053
  (Orders: Tel: (03) 347–0300)

British Library
Cataloguing in Publication Data
Inside the transputer. — (Computer
science texts).
  1. Multiprogramming microprocessor
systems
  I. Mitchell, David A. P.   II. Series
004'.32

  ISBN 0–632–01689–2

Library of Congress
Cataloging in Publication Data
Inside the transputer/David A. P. Mitchell . . .
    [et al.]. p. cm.—(Computer science texts)
    Includes bibliographical references.
    ISBN 0–632–01689–2
    1. Transputers.   I. Mitchell, David A. P.
    II. Series.
    TK7895.T73155 1990
    621.39'16—dc20

Contents

Preface

The transputer is a family of high performance microprocessors produced by INMOS Limited. One of its most significant features is the ability to perform multi-tasking in hardware, with sub-microsecond context switching. Communication between processes is also provided by hardware, both for internal data transfers, and transfers between different processors.

Unfortunately, there is a dearth of information regarding low-level aspects of the transputer. For a long time, INMOS claimed that since the transputer was specifically designed to efficiently execute the high-level language occam, it was not necessary for programmers to be aware of the machine-code instruction set. They have since had a change of heart, and have released *The Compiler Writer's Guide* [4], which describes the instruction set from the point of view of someone wishing to produce a compiler, as well as giving a brief formal definition of each instruction.

While *The Compiler Writer's Guide* is very good in what it sets out to achieve, it fails to show how the transputer works. For example, it is possible, using a short sequence of instructions, to make a process running on a transputer sleep while waiting for one of several events, such as input from a channel, or a particular time to come to pass. *The Compiler Writer's Guide* explains how to code such an instruction sequence; what it does not tell you is how this particular instruction sequence actually works. In this book, we have set out to fill this gap.

Chapter 1 gives an introduction to the transputer and occam, while chapter 2 describes the transputer's architecture.

Chapter 3 gives an overview of the instruction set. We have arranged this chapter from the point of view of a machine-code programmer, rather than a compiler writer. For example, all instructions that cause a branch or change in execution address are dealt with together, whereas in *The Compiler Writer's Guide* they would be dealt with under different categories, such as loops and procedure calls.

Chapter 4 contains many examples of programs written in machine-code, both to give a feel for assembly language programming, and to show some of the things that are impossible to do from occam.

Chapter 5 forms a reference section. Here, each transputer instruction is defined, one per page. We have included a formal definition for each instruction, which we have tried to make as readable as possible, whilst maintaining preciseness. There then follows an informal description of each instruction and finally, in most cases, a short example showing a typical use for that instruction.

Overall, we see this book as being complementary to, rather than in competition with, *The Compiler Writer's Guide*, and would recommend that the reader obtains a copy of that document too.

We have only included the 'core' transputer instructions in this book, that is to say, ones that are implemented on the T414. This has been done chiefly due to time and space considerations. Nevertheless, these instructions include amongst other things, all the process scheduling and communication instructions, which are the ones most in need of a detailed description.

The authors wish to acknowledge the assistance and encouragement of colleagues at both the Universities of Sheffield and Hull during the preparation of this book.

Finally, please note that INMOS and occam are trademarks of the INMOS group of companies.

Chapter 1

The Transputer

1.1 Background

In 1985 the transputer was first revealed to the world. At that time it was heralded as a revolution in computing. The first processor in the transputer series, the T414, boasted an unprecedented speed of 10 MIPS (millions of instructions per second), together with the ability to perform multitasking in hardware. Dedicated on-chip link controllers allowed for communications between processes running on different transputers, with minimal processor overhead. The T414 is a 32-bit processor with 2K of on-chip RAM and four interprocessor links, addressing up to 4Gbyte of external memory using multiplexed address and data lines.

Since then, various other members of the transputer family have been announced or released.

- The T212, a 16-bit version with 2K of onboard RAM and a 64K address range, using separate address and data buses.
- The M212, a T212 with two of the four links replaced by built-in disc controller circuitry.
- The T800, essentially a revamped T414 with a floating-point coprocessor integrated onto the chip, extra instructions, improved links and the onboard RAM doubled to 4K. This chip to a large extent has established the transputer's reputation, since it combines high performance floating-point processing (1.5 MFLOPs sustained) with the possibilities of parallel processing.
- The T222, a revamped T212 with 4K of onboard RAM.
- The T801, a T800 with separate address and data buses for faster memory accesses.

1

- The T425 and T805, upgraded versions of the T414 and T800 with extra instructions added to facilitate single-stepping, and other such debugging aids.

When the T414 was first released, INMOS decided to match the idiosyncratic nature of their new baby by their approach to marketing. For example, while trying to emphasise the novel and revolutionary aspects of their new processor, they more or less forgot to tell the general public that the T414 was in fact actually a microprocessor. An unusual and iconoclastic microprocessor perhaps, but a microprocessor nevertheless. Part of the problem was INMOS's insistence that the programming language, occam, was the "assembly language for the transputer", and that the transputer should always be programmed in occam.

occam is a high level language with strong support for parallel processing, and the transputer and occam were jointly developed with each other in mind. Consequently, occam programs compile to very compact, very efficient object code when the target processor is a transputer. This is quite a bit different from saying that occam is an "assembly language". Also, since the transputer is designed to execute compiled occam efficiently, it follows that it should work reasonably well with other high level languages, since occam has the same sorts of features such as loops, procedure calls and the like.

The consequences of INMOS's early approach meant that engineers were unable to run their beloved FORTRAN programs, and people wishing to use the transputer at a low level were denied use of assembly language. This last point is significant, since there are some things which simply cannot be done from occam—such as an idle time counter. This led to various groups of people (the authors included), poking around in the innards of the transputer, trying to ascertain what the various transputer instructions were, and what opcodes were associated with them. This soon led to a state of potential anarchy, with people making up their own mnemonics for each instruction, and often confusing instructions for similar-appearing ones (such as addition and indexing). Finally, INMOS relented, resulting in the release of *The Compiler Writer's Guide*, as well as FORTRAN, Pascal and C compilers.

1.2   The occam Language

Since the occam programming language is closely related to the transputer, and since some transputer instructions exist specifically to implement certain occam constructs, it is necessary to have at least a basic knowledge of occam to get the most out of this book. The rest of this chapter introduces the main features of occam; for more detailed coverage, the reader is referred to other books on the subject [1,2].

1.3 Processes and Concurrency

The transputer architecture uses processes as the fundamental standard software building block, and it provides the direct implementation of a process in hardware. A process is an independent computation which is able to communicate with other processes which are being executed at the same time. The communication between processes running on transputers is achieved by explicitly defined channels. A process itself can consist of subprocesses by time-sharing.

The transputer provides a number of links which support point-to-point communications between transputers, thereby enabling processes to be distributed over a network of transputers. Hence it is possible to program systems containing multiple interconnected transputers in which each transputer implements a set of processes. However it needs to be noted that the transputer can only communicate directly with another one to which it is physically wired. It is the ability to specify a hardwired function as an occam process which provides the architectural framework for transputers with specialised functions such as graphics.

When a pair of processes communicate with each other, one of the processes outputs a message to the channel and the other inputs the message from the same channel. The important point is that with these channels the communications are synchronised and unbuffered. When a channel is used to connect two processes, then the communication can only take place when both the input and output processes are ready. Whichever process reaches its input or output statement first, must wait until the other process is ready. Once both processes are ready then the inputting and outputting can proceed. This form of communication is equivalent to handshaking in other hardware systems. It provides the necessary level of process synchronisation.

A process may be ready to communicate on any number of channels. Communication takes place when another process is ready to communicate on one of the channels. Since the process itself may have internal concurrency, it may have many input channels and output channels performing communications at the same time.

1.4   occam Instructions

In occam, programs are built up from processes. Each process may
be regarded as a 'black box' with some particular internal state. The
processes are finite, such that each process starts, performs a number of
actions and then terminates. The simplest process is an action, and an
action consists of an assignment, an input or an output. Processes may
be combined together to form programs by way of process constructors.
Since each process may itself consist of other processes, some of which
may execute in parallel, the concept of processes as used in occam means
that there is a large amount of internal concurrency in the language. The
degree of concurrency that can actually be achieved at any given time
will alter as processes start and terminate.

Ultimately all processes are constructed from five primitive processes, namely:

(1) assignment,
(2) input,
(3) output,
(4) SKIP,
(5) STOP.

An assignment computes the value of an expression and sets a variable to this value. An assignment is indicated by the symbol :=. The
example

     b := e

sets the value of the variable b to the value of the expression e and then
terminates. Thus,

     y := 0

sets the value of y to zero.

Input is used for communicating between processes. Input is indicated by the symbol ?. In the example,

     d ? y

a value from the channel d is input and assigned to the variable y and
then the process terminates.

Like input, output is used for communicating between processes.
Output is indicated by the symbol !. In the example,

```
d ! e
```

the value of the expression *e* is output to the channel *d* and then the process terminates.

The SKIP process is a null process, that is, it simply terminates immediately without any further processing. On the other hand, the STOP process begins executing but never terminates.

A number of processes may be combined to form a construct. A construct is itself a process and so can be used to form part of a further construct. Each component process of a construct is written two spaces further from the left hand margin so as to indicate that it is part of the construct, and acts as a 'guard' for that particular construct. There are four main classes of construct:

(1) SEQ   sequential
(2) PAR   parallel
(3) IF   conditional
     WHILE   conditional
(4) ALT   alternative

The SEQ constructor specifies that the processes which follow are to be performed in a sequential manner, so that for example,

```
SEQ
  process1
  process2
```

means that *process1* is executed first, followed on its completion by *process2*. The whole sequence terminates when the last process, in this case *process2*, has itself terminated. It is again emphasised that in occam the level of indentation following a given constructor is important, and consists of two spaces. This specifies the range of that constructor and acts as a guard for those processes.

In the example,

```
SEQ
  c1 ? x
  x := x + 1
  c2 ! x
```

a value is input on channel *c1* and assigned to the variable *x*. Then *x* is incremented by 1, and finally the result is output on channel *c2*.

To provide concurrency, the constructor PAR means that processes are executed in parallel. For example,

```
PAR
    process1
    process2
```

means that *process1* and *process2* execute in parallel with each other. The processes must be independent of each other, and the construct terminates only after all the component processes have terminated; but there is no fixed order in which the individual processes will terminate. For example,

```
PAR
    c1 ? x
    c2 ! y
```

allows the communication of input on channel *c1* of the variable x, and output on the channel *c2* of the variable y to take place together, i.e. concurrently. This parallelism is highly optimised so as to incur minimal process scheduling.

There also exists a conditional construct:

```
IF
    condition1
        process1
    condition2
        process2
    . . .
```

where *condition1* and *condition2* represent conditions whose values may be either *true* or *false*. This construct is such that *process1* will be executed if *condition1* is *true*, otherwise *process2* is executed if *condition2* is *true*, and so on. Only one of the processes is executed, and then the construct terminates. For example,

```
IF
    x = 0
        y := y + 1
    TRUE
        SKIP
```

increments the value of the variable y only if x is zero. It is important in this construct that at least one of the conditions is *true*, or the construct will behave as a STOP and the process will halt. In the above example this criteria is provided by the use of the SKIP.

Another form of conditional construct is that of the WHILE construct. In this construct,

```
WHILE condition
    process
```

the process is continuously executed until the value of the condition is false. For example,

```
WHILE x > 5
    x := x - 5
```

leaves x with the value of (x remainder 5) if x is positive.

A further construct is the ALT, or alternative, which provides a selection between processes. The ALT construct takes the list of processes within its guard and performs the first process that it finds which satisfies its appropriate guard condition. For example,

```
ALT
    guard1
        process1
    guard2
        process2
    guard3
        process3
    ...
```

waits until one of the guard conditions *guard1*, *guard2* or *guard3* is ready. A guard condition consists of an event to wait for, such as channel input, plus an optional boolean value. (If this value is *false*, then the guard is ignored.) If *guard1* is ready first then *process1* proceeds, similarly if *guard2* becomes ready first then *process2* will be executed, and so on. Only one process will be executed, and then the ALT process terminates when the process which has been chosen itself terminates. Note that if all the guards have their optional boolean value set to *false*, then the ALT construct behaves as a STOP. An example ALT construct is,

```
ALT
    (counter < max) & chan ? data
        SEQ
            sum:= sum + data
            counter := counter + 1
    total ? signal
```

```
      SEQ
        out ! sum/counter
        counter := 0
        sum := 0
    TRUE & SKIP
      SKIP
```

which undertakes one of the following:

(1) when there is data on channel *chan* and the counter is less than some limit *max*, inputs *data*, adds it to *sum* and increments a count, *counter*, or

(2) when there is a signal on the channel *total*, outputs on the channel *out* the average of the data read in, and resets the variables *counter* and *sum*, or

(3) does nothing

In addition to the constructs which have been discussed so far, a replicator may be used with a constructor in order to repeat a process a number of times. For example,

```
    SEQ i = 0 FOR n
      process1
```

causes *process1* to be repeated *n* times. Or, for a parallel construct,

```
    PAR i = 0 FOR n
      process(i)
```

constructs an array of *n* similar processes, $process(0)$, $process(1)$, ..., $process(n - 1)$.

A replicated ALT construct also exists which consists of a number of identically structured alternatives, each of which is triggered by input from a channel. For example, a multiplexer might be provided by,

```
    [20] CHAN OF INT In:
    CHAN OF INT Out:
    PAR
      ... processes providing data on In channels
      WHILE TRUE
        INT y:
        ALT i = 0 FOR 20
          In[i] ? y
            Out ! y
      ... processes taking data from out channel
```

This example monitors 20 input channels *In*, and when any one has any data, then the data from the appropriate *In* channel, is passed to the *Out* channel. Hence communication from the 20 *In* channels is merged into the *Out* channel.

In occam, every variable, expression and value has a type, which may be a primitive or an array type. The type defines the length and interpretations of the type. The following are the types which are present in all implementations of occam:

CHAN   Each communication channel provides one way communication between two concurrent processes

TIMER   Each timer provides a clock which can be used by any number of concurrent processes

INT   INT is a signed integer whose range is chosen by the compiler to be easily implementable on the target machine.

              In addition, it is possible to specify explicit integer ranges:

                INT16 $-32768\ldots32767$
                INT32 $-2147483648\ldots2147483647$
                INT64 $-2^{63}\ldots2^{63}-1$

REAL32 Floating point numbers using a sign bit, 8 bit exponent and 23 bit mantissa

REAL64 Floating point numbers using a sign bit, 11 bit exponent and 52 bit mantissa.

A variable, expression or value may be declared to be one of the above types by use of a declaration of the form

```
T x :
```

meaning that x has been declared to be of type T, where T may be a new channel, variable or timer. The declaration is terminated by the use of a colon. For example,

```
INT x :
process1
```

declares x as an integer to be used in *process1*.

Array types are constructed from components. For example,

```
[n] T
```

is an array constructed from n components of type T. A component of an array may be selected by subscription, so that,

```
v[e]
```

selects the component e of array v. A set of components of an array may also be selected by subscription. For example,

```
[v FROM e FOR c]
```

selects the components $v[e]$, $v[e+1],\ldots,v[e+c-1]$.

It is often useful to be able to refer to a process by name. This may be done using the definition PROC. For example,

```
PROC square (VAL INT n, INT sqr)
   sqr := n * n
 :
```

defines the name of the process square. This may be referred to elsewhere in the program. For example,

```
square (x,sqrx)
```

means

```
sqrx := x * x
```

In the discussion so far, several operators have been assumed to exist, such as +, -, and *. The operators which are available in occam are given below.

Operator	Operand type	Description
+,-,*,/	integer, real	arithmetic operators
PLUS,MINUS,TIMES,AFTER	integer	modulo arithmetic
=,<>	any primitive	relational operators
>,<,>=,<=	integer, real	relational operators
AND, OR, NOT	boolean	boolean operators
BITAND,BITOR,><,BITNOT	integer	bit operators
<<,>>	integer	shift operators

In the previous section, the provision of interprocess-communication through occam channels was discussed. These channels provide point-to-point communications which ensure that messages are both synchronised and unbuffered. By this means the requirement of process synchronisation is ensured within the language itself. We can illustrate such synchronisation in the consideration of a simple queue. The program considers data as flowing down a pipeline represented as a series of slots, where the slots form an array of parallel processors which pass data between adjacent slots. A simple approach to this might be:

```
[20] CHAN OF INT slot:
PAR i := 0 FOR 19
  WHILE TRUE
    INT y:
    SEQ
      slot[i] ? y
      slot[i+1] ! y
```

Here we define an array *slot* of 20 channels, and use a replicated PAR construct so that 19 parallel processes are set up which continually transfer data between adjacent slots in the queue. The synchronisation between successive slots is achieved by the SEQ construct. However it should be noted that this represents only a fragment of a program, and in particular it does not provide a mechanism for input into *slot*[0], or any effective output for data from *slot*[19].

Chapter 2

Transputer Hardware Description

2.1 Introduction

The transputer is a high performance microprocessor which has been designed to facilitate interprocess and interprocessor communication. The transputer architecture defines a family of programmable VLSI components which include the T212, T414 and a floating-point processor, the T800. In this text we shall only be considering the T414, but the general features of the transputer architecture are given in figure 2.1, and apply to the other members of the family. The principal features include:

- Processor
- On-chip static Random Access Memory (RAM)
- External memory controller
- Hardware time-slicing
- High-speed serial links (INMOS Links)

The T414 transputer is basically a 32-bit processor which has 2 Kbytes of static RAM and four communication links integrated onto a single chip in a CMOS process. Memory is extensible off chip with the total addressing range being 4 gigabytes (2^{32}). The data path to the memory is a full 32 bits wide, and configurable strobes are supplied that allow direct interfacing to dynamic RAM.

The processor itself is rated, for the standard 20 MHz part, at 10 MIPs (million instructions per second). The processor provides di-

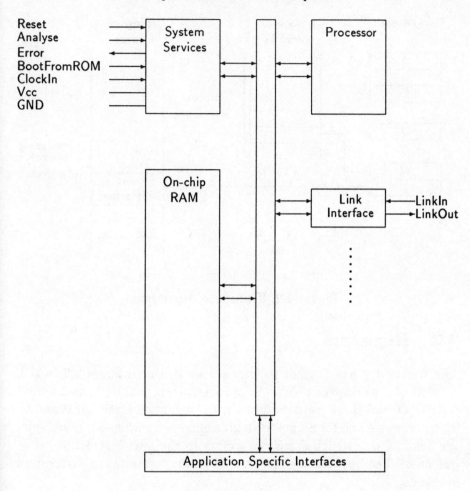

Figure 2.1. Transputer architecture.

rect hardware support for the occam model of concurrency, with sub-microsecond context switching, and two levels of process priority.

Communication with other processors or through link adaptor chips, to the outside world is provided by four independent, bi-directional IN-MOS serial links. These links run at bit rates of 5, 10 or 20 Mbps (million bits per second) and have DMA (Direct Memory Access) interfaces into memory to allow the transfer of messages to take place with the minimum of processor intervention. In addition, a single interrupt input, which is called the *event*, allows external circuitry to control a process.

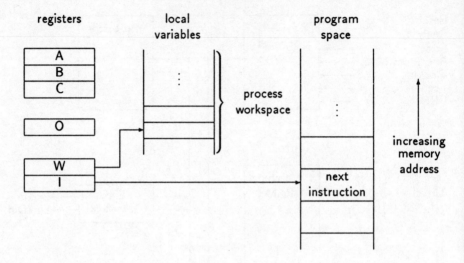

Figure 2.2. Transputer registers.

2.2   Registers

The transputer has a small register set as shown in figure 2.2, which consists of a workspace pointer W, an instruction pointer I, an operand register O, and three registers forming an evaluation stack: A, B and C. The workspace pointer points to an area of memory where local variables are held. The instruction pointer points to the next instruction to be executed. The operand register is used in the formation of instruction operands.

Registers A, B and C are sources and destinations for most arithmetic and logical operations. Loading a value onto the evaluation stack pushes B into C, and A into B, before loading A. Storing a value from A pops B into A and C into B. Expressions are evaluated on the evaluation stack, and instructions refer to the stack implicitly.

In addition to these six registers, there are four registers which handle the two active process queues, namely *Fptr0*, *Fptr1*, *Bptr0* and *Bptr1*, and two timer registers *Time0* and *Time1*. There are two single-bit flags for dealing with errors, *Error* and *HaltOnError*. In addition, the first few locations in internal memory are used for specific purposes.

The two timer registers *Time0* and *Time1* consist of a low priority timer which increments every 64 microseconds, and a high priority timer which increments every 1 microsecond. A single time slice lasts for 1024 high priority time periods, and low priority processes are descheduled at

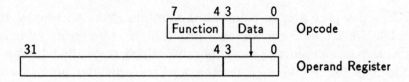

Figure 2.3. Instruction format.

the first opportunity after two time slice periods have been completed. High priority processes are never pre-empted.

When a process is timesliced out, the value of its instruction pointer I, is stored just below the current local workspace, i.e. one word below the address pointed to by the workspace pointer W. In addition, the process is linked to the back of the high or low priority active process queue. On the other hand, if a process becomes halted as a result of channel communication, then its instruction pointer is still stored, but in addition, its workspace pointer is placed in the word of memory allocated to the channel. When another process tries to communicate on the channel, i.e. attempts to access the channel word, the halted process is relinked to the back of the relevant active queue.

The instruction format of the transputer has been optimised for minimum code space requirements. Each instruction consists of a single 8-bit byte which is split into two 4-bit values, making up a function and operand. This is shown in figure 2.3.

2.3 The Workspace Pointer

The workspace pointer holds an address. An address in general consists of two parts, a word selector and a byte offset within that word. The bottom few bits of the address form the byte offset, and the rest form the word selector. In the case of a 32-bit transputer such as a T414 or T800, two byte offset bits are used, allowing byte offsets 0,1,2 and 3.

The workspace pointer W is a one word wide register whose byte offset bits are set to zero, so that it always points to a word boundary in memory. The least significant bit is used instead to store the process priority, which is zero for a high priority process, and one for low priority. The combination of workspace address and priority bit is referred to as a *process descriptor*.

The workspace pointer points to the bottom of the workspace. It is used like a stack on a conventional processor to store return addresses and local variables during procedure calls. (Using conventional compiler terminology, we would say that the workspace pointer points to the base of the current stack frame.) This stack grows downwards towards more negative addresses, with local variables being accessed by positive offsets from W. As will be explained shortly, the way that transputer instructions are coded means that variables which are stored at small positive offsets from the workspace pointer can be accessed using very short instruction sequences.

In addition, few words of memory just below the workspace pointer are used by the various parts of the scheduling hardware. In general, these are only used when the process is descheduled, so the value of the workspace pointer may be altered at any time by the programmer without harm being caused. The only exception to this is during the sequence of instructions that implements the selection part of an ALT construct, where W should be left undisturbed. The locations used are as follows, specified relative to W:

-1 holds the instruction pointer of a descheduled process
-2 used to maintain a list of active, but descheduled processes
-3 used during channel communication to hold the address of data to be transferred
-4 flag used during timer ALTs to indicate a valid time to wait for
-5 used during timer ALTs to hold the time to wait for

Appendix C gives a more detailed description of the use of these locations, and shows what values each location may hold under various conditions.

2.4   The Instruction Pointer

The instruction pointer I, is the transputer's program counter. It points to the byte in memory that contains the next instruction to be executed. Instructions are actually read from memory a word at a time into an instruction pipeline buffer from where the processor takes them as required. This means that for a 32-bit processor, four instructions are read in a single cycle.

On the T414, the pipeline can hold 8 instructions, that is two 32-bit words. Since it takes no more than two memory cycles to fill, the number of memory cycles wasted by fetching unnecessary instructions when a branch is taken is only one, since one cycle is needed to fetch the branch instruction itself.

Unlike a conventional processor, the transputer has an instruction pointer value associated with each process. When a process is descheduled, this value is stored just below the current workspace, and when the process becomes the running process it is transferred back to the instruction pointer. As only one process can run at a time there needs to be only one instruction pointer register. The mechanism described enables the transputer to appear to run several processes simultaneously.

2.5 The Operand Register

The operand register O, is a one word wide register which is used for assembling the operand of an instruction from the 4-bit data fragments supplied. All instructions place the contents of their 4-bit operand field into the least significant four bits of the operand register, moving the existing contents 4 bits to the left. The register is then used as the operand for the function which is specified by the other 4-bit field of the instruction.

Instructions normally clear the operand register after they have executed. However, a Prefix instruction exists which does nothing, except shift its four bits of operand left into the operand register, leaving this register uncleared after execution. Thus by using a series of Prefix instructions before a proper instruction, the range of that instruction's operand may be extended to as many bits as required. There is also a Negative Prefix instruction which complements the contents of the operand register after shifting.

Finally, there is an Operate instruction, which uses its operand as an opcode number, giving the transputer access to a further set of instructions above the basic 16 which are allowed for by the instruction format. Since the operand of the operate instruction may itself be extended by prefixing, the transputer can have an arbitrary number of instructions. The only proviso is that only 16 of them may actually have immediate operands (or 13, once Prefix, Negative Prefix and Operate are accounted for); the rest must have implicit operands. As an example, the ADD instruction adds the top two elements of the evaluation stack together,

Data	1	1	D0	D1	D2	D3	D4	D5	D6	D7	0

Acknowledge	1	0

Figure 2.4. Link protocol.

leaving the result on the stack.

2.6   Communications Links

One of the aims of the transputer architecture is to provide a family
of compatible components that can communicate with each other using the minimal amount of external logic, irrespective of the individual
internal clock rates. To achieve this each transputer can communicate
via point-to-point links called INMOS links, using an asynchronous bit-
serial protocol. Each transputer has a fixed number of such links, typically four; each of the links is bi-directional, and a variety of topologies
can be configured using these links. For example, pairs of transputers
may be connected together as a doublet, and then this doublet with its
associated six links can be placed at each vertex of a cubic lattice.

The messages themselves are transmitted as a sequence of data packets, each of which must be acknowledged by an acknowledge packet.
Each link consists of a pair of channels, one in each direction. Data
packets for one direction are multiplexed on the same wire with acknowledge packets that are associated with messages for the other direction.
The acknowledge packets are used both to signal reception of the data
packets and to maintain flow control. The link protocol for the INMOS
links is shown in figure 2.4. Transputer links themselves are formed by
the interconnection of the *LinkIn* and *LinkOut* signals on the relevant
transputers. Since the link protocol is asynchronous, the relative skew,
which is typically caused by the different rising and falling edge times
of the link signals, must be kept within tolerance. This needs careful
consideration in its implication for certain interconnection topologies.

From the programmer's point of view there is no difference between
sending a message between two processes running on separate transputers over a hardware link, and two processes running on the same
transputer. In all cases, the programmer specifies an address in memory, called the channel word. Hardware determines whether the com-

munication is internal or external, based on the address of the word.
The conventional names and addresses for the channels associated with
hardware links in the T414 are:

```
PLACE Link0Output AT #80000000:
PLACE Link1Output AT #80000004:
PLACE Link2Output AT #80000008:
PLACE Link3Output AT #8000000C:
PLACE Link0Input  AT #80000010:
PLACE Link1Input  AT #80000014:
PLACE Link2Input  AT #80000018:
PLACE Link3Input  AT #8000001C:
```

Each data packet as shown in figure 2.4 consists of a 'one' bit followed
by another 'one' bit, followed by eight data bits followed by a zero bit.
After transmitting a data packet, the sender transputer waits until an
acknowledge is received, which signifies that the receiving transputer is
ready to receive another packet. The acknowledge consists of two data
bits, the first being a one and the second being a zero.

The receiving transputer can send an acknowledge as soon as the data
packet has been identified, so that communications can be continuous,
provided that there is sufficient buffer space for another data packet,
and the inputting process is ready to receive the previous data packet.
This protocol synchronises the communications of each byte of data.
The communication is independent of word length, so that transputers
using different word lengths can communicate directly.

Link selection pins on the transputer allow some selection of link
speeds. Link speeds can be set by *LinkSpecial*, *Link0Special* and *Link-
123Special*. Link 0 can be set independently. In the table below, the values for the unidirectional and bidirectional data rates are given. *Linkn-
Special* is to be taken as *Link0Special* when selecting link 0 speed and
as *Link123Special* for the others. All these rates are assuming that the
transputer is using internal memory.

Link- *Special*	*Linkn-* *Special*	Mbits/sec	Kbytes/sec (T414) unidirectional	bidirectional
0	0	10	400	800
0	1	5	200	400
1	0	10	400	800
1	1	20	800	1600

The INMOS links may be interfaced to peripherals via an INMOS link adapter, which converts a serial link into an 8-bit parallel port. Additionally, the transputer provides an input pin, *EventReq* and an output pin, *EventAck* which provide interrupt facilities. A peripheral may signal an interrupt to the transputer via the *EventReq* pin, which the transputer acknowledges using *EventAck*. Internally, the transputer makes available a special hardware channel which behaves as if a synchronising message has been received on each low to high transition of the *EventReq* pin. A process may wait on this 'channel', in which case it serves as an interrupt handler. An occam channel may be associated with the *EventReq* pin by a channel association. The conventional name and the address used for this channel are:

```
PLACE Event AT #80000020:
```

Event then behaves like an ordinary channel, and an occam process may synchronise with a low to high transition on the *EventReq* pin by using the occam construct

```
Event ? signal
```

The process then waits until the channel *Event* is ready. If the process waiting on the channel is high priority, then it will interrupt any low priority process running when *EventReq* goes from low to high.

2.7   Communication Protocol

Communication over both internal and external channels is essentially byte orientated. The instructions concerned are IN, OUT, OUTWORD and OUTBYTE.

Communication over internal channels observes the following protocol. Before any communication is attempted, the channel word must be initialised to contain *MinInt*. This operation is done when the channel is declared and space is reserved for the channel word. When an input or output is subsequently attempted, the channel word is inspected: if it contains *MinInt*, then the process descriptor of the current process is placed in the channel word and the process is descheduled. In this case the instruction pointer and the address of the message to be transferred are stored at locations which have offsets of −1 and −3 relative to the workspace pointer, respectively. If however, the content of the channel word is not *MinInt*, thereby indicating that the other process involved is already waiting to communicate, then the communication may be performed.

The communication itself is achieved by copying the required block of data from the source to the destination. This is possible since the data address is available through the process descriptor stored in the channel word. Once the transfer is completed, the process that arrived first and was descheduled, is rescheduled and the channel word is reset to contain *MinInt*.

External links behave in a similar manner. The only difference as far as software is concerned is that the control word of an external link is at one of the addresses #80000000 to #8000001C rather than an arbitrary address in memory. The same instructions are used for input and output on both external links and internal channels.

2.8   Errors

High-level language execution is made secure with, for example, array bound checking and arithmetic overflow detection. If the compiler is unable to check that a given construct contains only valid expressions and processes, then extra instructions are compiled in order to perform the necessary check at runtime. If the result of this check indicates that an error has occurred then the processor's *Error* flag is set. This error can be handled either internally by software, or externally by using the *Error* pin. It is also possible, by setting the *HaltOnError* flag, to make the processor halt if the *Error* flag ever gets set. If the processor halts as a result of an error, then the links will continue with any outstanding transfers, the memory continues to provide refresh cycles and the transputer may be analysed.

When a high priority process pre-empts a low priority process then the status of the *Error* and *HaltOnError* Flags, and all the registers are saved in internal RAM in the area below *MemStart* for the duration of the high priority process, and restored at the conclusion of it. The status of the *Error* flag is transmitted to the high priority process, but the *HaltOnError* flag is cleared before the process starts. Either flag can be altered in the process without upsetting the error status of the pre-empted low priority process. When there are no high priority processes to run, then the current state of the *Error* flag is lost and the preserved state is restored, as part of commencing to execute the pre-empted low priority process.

In the event of the transputer halting because of the *HaltOnError* flag, the links will finish outstanding transfers before shutting down. If the *Analyse* pin is asserted, then all inputs continue, but outputs will not make another access to memory for data.

After halting due to the *Error* flag becoming set whilst *HaltOnError* is set, the instruction pointer points to two bytes past the instruction which set the *Error* flag. After halting due to *Analyse* being taken high, the instruction pointer points one byte past the instruction which is being executed. In both of these cases the instruction pointer will be copied into the A register.

2.9   Time

Timing in occam is provided by use of a timer channel which can only provide input. The value which is input is the current time, which is represented as an integer value. The cycle of the clock depends on the wordsize, on the amount by which the reading is incremented at each clock tick and on the frequency of the clock ticks. Each of these parameters will depend on the particular implementation of the hardware on which the occam program is running. In the transputer, the clock ticks for low priority processes are in units of (input clockrate)/(5*64), which normally works out at 64 microseconds per tick. With a 64 microsecond tick and a 16-bit integer, then the cycle time would be approximately 4.2 seconds; with a 32-bit integer the corresponding cycle time would be approximately 76 hours.

The processor has timers to support two levels of priority. The priority 1 (low priority) processes are executed whenever there are no active priority 0 (high priority) processes. High priority processes are expected to execute for short time intervals. If one or more such processes can proceed, then one is selected and allowed to execute until it has to wait for a communication, a timer input, or until the process is completed. However, if no high priority process is able to proceed and one or more low priority processes are able to proceed, then one of the low priority processes is selected. Low priority processes are time-sliced to provide an even distribution of the processor time between computationally intensive tasks. If there are n low priority processes, then the maximum latency, expressed as the time from when a low priority process becomes active to the time at which it starts processing is $(2n-2)$ time-slice periods. The low priority timer increments every 64 microseconds, whereas the high priority timer increments every 1 microsecond. A single time-slice period lasts for 1024 high priority time periods. In order to ensure that low priority processes do proceed, high priority processes must not continuously occupy the processor for a period equal to that of a time slice. If a low priority process is waiting for an external channel to become ready, and there are no active high priority processes, then the interrupt latency, which is the time interval from when the channel becomes ready until the process starts executing, is typically 19 processor cycles, though it may extend to a maximum of 58 cycles, all assuming the use of on-chip RAM.

2.10   Reset, Analyse and Booting

The system services comprise the clocks, power and initialisation used by the whole of the transputer. The *Reset* and *Analyse* input pins enable the transputer to be initialised or halted in a way which preserves its state for subsequent analysis. While the transputer is running, both *Reset* and *Analyse* are held low. The transputer is initialised by pulsing *Reset* high whilst holding *Analyse* low. Operation ceases immediately and all current state information is lost. When *Reset* goes low the transputer sets up the memory interface configuration as appropriate. The processor and links start operating after the memory interface configuration cycle is complete and sufficient refresh cycles have been executed to initialise any dynamic RAM. The processor then bootstraps.

The transputer can be bootstrapped either from a link or from external ROM. If *BootFromRom* is connected high, then the transputer starts to execute code from the top two bytes in external memory, at address #7FFFFFFE. This location should contain a backward jump to a program in ROM. The processor is in a low priority state. The workspace register points to *MemStart*, which is where the user memory begins and is at address location #80000048 for the T414.

If *BootFromRom* is connected low, the transputer will wait for the first bootstrap message to arrive on any one of its serial links. The transputer itself is ready to receive the first, or control byte, on the link within two processor cycles after *Reset* goes low. If the control byte received is greater than 1, then it is taken as the number of bytes to be input. The following bytes, up to this specified number, are then placed in internal memory starting at location *MemStart*. Following the receipt of the last byte, the transputer will start executing code at *MemStart* as a low priority process. The memory space immediately above the loaded code is used as workspace. Messages arriving on other links after the control byte has been received, or on the bootstrapping link after the last bootstrap byte, will be retained until a process inputs from the appropriate link.

The other options for the value of the control byte are 0 and 1, and use of these values allow the facility to 'peek' and 'poke'. Any location in either internal or external memory can be interrogated and altered when the transputer is waiting to boot from a link. If the control byte is 0 then eight more bytes are expected on the same link. The first 4 byte word is taken as an internal or external memory address at which to poke, i.e. write, the second 4 byte word. If the control byte is 1 the next four bytes are used as the address from which to peek, i.e. read, a word of data—this data word is sent down the output channel of the same link. After a peek or poke operation, the transputer returns to its previously held state. There is no limit to the number of peek and poke operations that may take place before the control byte has a value greater than 1, when the transputer will then begin to read its bootstrap code. When performing the peek and poke operations, any of the links may be used except that the addresses and data must be transmitted via the same link as that of the control byte.

When initialising after power-on, a time is specified during which the 5V supply, Vcc, must be within specification, *Reset* must be high, and the input on *ClockIn* must be oscillating. *Reset* is taken low after this specified time has elapsed.

In order to analyse a system following a reset, the first step is for the *Analyse* pin to be taken high. This causes the transputer to halt within three time-slice periods, approximately 3 milliseconds, plus the time taken for any high priority process to stop processing. Any outputting links continue to operate until they complete the remainder of the current word. Input links continue to receive data. Provided that there are no delays in sending acknowledgements, the links in the system will therefore cease activity within a few microseconds. Sufficient time must be allowed both for the processor to halt and for all the link traffic to be completed before *Reset* is asserted. The memory interface is not affected by *Analyse*, or *Reset* while *Analyse* is held high. If refresh cycles are enabled, then it continues to refresh external dynamic RAM.

After the end of a valid *reset* or *analyse* sequence, the processor's registers are initialised to specific values, depending on how the processor was started up. These values are as follows:

W   *MemStart* if bootstrapping from ROM, or the address of the first free word after a bootstrap program if bootstrapping from link.

I   *MemStart* if bootstrapping from a link, or the external memory bootstrap address (#7FFFFFFE) if bootstrapping from ROM.

A   The value of I when the processor halted.

B   The value of W when the processor halted, together with the priority of the process when the transputer halted.

C   The identity of the bootstrapping link if bootstrapping from a link.

Chapter 3

Instruction Set Overview

The T414 has exactly one hundred instructions. These can be broken down as follows:

- 16 addressing and memory access,
- 41 arithmetic and logical,
- 6 branching and program control,
- 12 process scheduling and control,
- 16 inter-process communication,
- 9 miscellaneous.

It is interesting to note that instructions for dealing with concurrency amount to over a quarter of the total, or nearly five times the number of branching and program control instructions!

This chapter is designed to give an overview of the instruction set, with each instruction discussed within one of the groupings mentioned above. A more detailed explanation of each instruction will be found in the reference section of this book (Chapter 5).

3.1 Addressing and Memory Access

The transputer provides two main ways of addressing memory: addresses may be specified as a fixed offset from an address held in either the workspace pointer, or in the A register. The former is referred to as local access, since the workspace pointer conventionally points to an area of memory used to hold the local variables for a procedure. In fact, the first few words in memory offset from the workspace pointer are often referred to as 'local 0', 'local 1' etc. Conversely, access via the A register is called non-local.

Instructions are provided to read and write words from memory using the above addressing scheme; also provided are instructions to read and write bytes, to move a block of bytes, to perform word-length independent addressing calculations, to modify the value of the workspace pointer, and finally to specify an address relative to the instruction pointer.

3.1.1 Loading and Storing

The transputer provides the following general-purpose instructions for loading and storing words in memory:

LDL n	Load Local
STL n	Store Local
LDNL n	Load Non-Local
STNL n	Store Non-Local

LDL n loads a word onto the evaluation stack (i.e. into the A register) which lies offset n words from the address pointed to by the workspace pointer, where n is the instruction's operand. The original value in A is pushed into B, and B into C. STL n performs the reverse, storing the value of the A register at the specified address. LDNL n and STNL n are similar, except that that they use the A register as the base address, rather than the workspace pointer. LDNL n loads the word into the A register, overwriting the address already stored there, while STNL n stores the value contained in the B register, afterwards popping both A and B.

LDLP n	Load Local Pointer
LDNLP n	Load Non-Local Pointer

are similar to the previous instructions, except that they store in A the effective address that is calculated, rather than the value of the word stored at that address. This is useful for subsequent instructions which require an address on the stack as one of their operands.

3.1.2 Byte Accesses

The transputer normally accesses memory a word at a time; however, it can be persuaded to access individual bytes with the next three instructions:

LB	Load Byte
SB	Store Byte
MOVE	Move Message

LB loads the byte at the address contained in the A register into the A register, overwriting its previous contents. Unlike word addressing, the bottom couple of bits of the address, which form the byte offset, are used to select a particular byte from within the word. SB stores a byte contained in the bottom eight bits of B at the address pointed to by A. Finally, MOVE copies a block of bytes from the address in C to the address in B, the number of bytes to move specified in A. The MOVE instruction is intelligent enough to read or write a word's worth of bytes in a single cycle wherever possible.

3.1.3   Addressing Arithmetic

The two instructions

WSUB	Word Subscript
BSUB	Byte Subscript

allow indexing of arrays, or their equivalents. WSUB increments the address in the A register by the number of words specified in the B register, whereas BSUB increments it by the number of bytes. The existence of these instructions allows address arithmetic to be word-length independent; for example on the T414, the returned value of WSUB is equivalent to $a + 4b$, while the T212 would return $a + 2b$.

Two further instructions,

WCNT	Word Count
BCNT	Byte Count

are provided for word-length independent addressing. WCNT breaks the address in the A register into its word address and byte offset components, storing the two values in A and B, while BCNT multiplies the value in A by the number of bytes in a word. This would be useful in calculating the number of bytes in an array of words for a (byte oriented) MOVE command, for example.

3.1.4   Other Addressing Instructions

There are two instructions that modify the value of the workspace pointer:

AJW n   Adjust Workspace
GAJW   General Adjust Workspace

AJW n increments the workspace pointer by the number of words specified by its operand n (or decrements if n is negative). This instruction is most commonly used at the beginning and end of a procedure call, to allocate some more stack space and then relinquish it. Since the stack normally grows down in memory, the usual sequence of instructions would be AJW -k; ...; AJW +k, where k is the number of extra words to allocate.

GAJW is a more general instruction, which simply exchanges the contents of the workspace pointer and the A register.

Finally, the instruction

LDPI   Load Pointer To Instruction

calculates an address, which consists of the current value of the instruction pointer (which always points to the next instruction), incremented by the number of *bytes* specified by the value in the A register. This address then replaces the value in A. So, LDC 2; LDPI would leave an address in A which points two bytes on from the instruction following the LDPI. This is very useful for producing relocatable code, since a program's data can be specified relative to its code.

3.2   Arithmetic and Logical

The three simplest instructions are

REV   Reverse
LDC n   Load Constant
MINT   Minimum Integer

It could be argued that these are not really arithmetic instructions; however, this is the most convenient place to discuss them. REV simply swaps the contents of the top two elements of the evaluation stack, i.e. the A and B registers. LDC pushes the constant specified by its operand onto the evaluation stack, that is to say, storing it in the A register, pushing A onto B, B onto C, and losing the value in C. Finally, MINT pushes the constant *MinInt* onto the evaluation stack; this is a single-word value with the top bit set to 1 and all other bits to 0. This instruction is word-length independent. It is very useful, especially for channel communication (see later).

3.2.1 Single Length Arithmetic

Next there is the

     ADC n   Add Constant

instruction, which adds its operand to the value in the A register, rather than just pushing it.

Then there are a group of eight arithmetic operators which take their operands from the A and B registers, leaving the result in the A register.

     ADD   Signed Addition
     SUB   Signed Subtraction
     MUL   Multiply
     DIV   Divide
     REM   Remainder

all perform signed single-length arithmetic, with the error flag being set on overflow, whereas

     SUM   Unsigned Addition
     DIFF   Unsigned Subtraction
     PROD   Unsigned Multiplication

are similar, except that carry and overflow are ignored. Finally,

     FMUL   Fractional Multiply

multiplies two single-word values together, but gives as its answer the high word of the result (more or less), rather than the low, as in MUL.

3.2.2 Comparing

There are two main comparison instructions.

     EQC n   Equals Constant

compares the value of the A register with the operand. If they are equal, *true* (1) is stored in A, else *false* (0) is stored.

     GT   Greater Than

compares the values in the A and B registers; if B is greater than A, then it returns *true* in the A register. Together with the logical/bitwise instructions discussed next, these two instructions can evaluate all the various types of arithmetic comparison. This is an example of where the transputer has the flavour of a RISC processor.

There are a further two comparison instructions which are designed mainly to check the range of array subscripts:

CSUB0   Check Subscript From Zero
CCNT1   Check Count From One

Both these instructions check the range of the value in the B register, and if it is outside, set the error flag. The range is specified by the value of the A register; for CSUB0, the valid range is $0 \ldots a$; for CCNT1, the valid range is $1 \ldots a$.

3.2.3   Bit Operators

There are six bitwise operators.

AND   Bitwise AND
OR   Bitwise OR
XOR   Bitwise Exclusive-OR

perform boolean operations between corresponding bits in the A and B registers.

NOT   Complement

complements every bit in the A register, while

SHL   Shift Left
SHR   Shift Right

both shift the value in the B register left or right by the number of places specified by the A register, filling the extra bits with zeros.

3.2.4   Multiple Word Arithmetic

There are versions of most of the above arithmetic instructions designed to deal with multiple word-length data.

LADD   Long Add
LSUM   Long Sum
LSUB   Long Subtract
LDIFF   Long Difference

have the same effect as their single-word counterparts, except that a single bit carry or borrow is contained in the C register. LSUM and LDIFF are used for the low order words of the calculation, while LADD and LSUB are used for the top word, since they perform overflow checking.

LMUL   Long Multiply

multiplies the values in the A and B registers together and adds in the 'carry' in the C register. The double word result is stored in the A and B registers, the high word in B. The value in B thus becomes the carry-in for higher order words.

> LDIV   Long Divide

divides the double-length word in register pair BA by the value in C, storing the integer result in A and the remainder in B. Note that to avoid overflow, B must be less than C.

The two instructions

> LSHL   Long Shift Left
> LSHR   Long Shift Right

shift the double word value contained in register pair BA a number of places specified by the C register, filling the extra bits with zeros.

Finally,

> XDBLE   Extend To Double
> CSNGL   Check Single

convert a single word value into a double word value and vice versa. CSNGL sets the error flag if the value cannot be squeezed into a single word.

3.2.5   Partword Arithmetic

Partword arithmetic (that is to say, using signed numbers represented by less bits than there are in a word) is supported by the two instructions

> XWORD   Extend To Word
> CWORD   Check Word.

The idea is that partword values are first sign-extended to full words using XWORD; normal arithmetic operations are then carried out, and the result is checked with CWORD, which sets the error flag if the value is out of the partword range.

3.2.6   Floating-Point Support

The instruction

> NORM   Normalise

normalises the double word value in BA by shifting it left until the top bit is set. The number of places shifted left is stored in C.

There are a further set of instructions

CFLERR	Check Floating Point Infinity or Not-a-Number
LDINF	Load Single Length Infinity
POSTNORMSN	Post-Normalise Correction
ROUNDSN	Round Single Length Floating Point Number
UNPACKSN	Unpack Single Length Floating Point Number

which are specific to the T414, and are designed to provide hardware support for (software) floating-point packages. For obvious reasons they have not been included in the floating-point T800 transputer. Incidentally, it is the existence of these instructions that gives the T414 a floating-point performance which is comparable to processors with dedicated floating-point co-processors (such as the 68020/68881 combination).

3.3 Branching and Program Control

The transputer provides only six instructions for altering the flow of control of the program. In this respect, it again comes close to being a RISC processor.

3.3.1 Branching

The three instructions

CJ n	Conditional Jump
J n	Jump
LEND	Loop End

provide branching. CJ n examines the value in the A register. If it is *false* (0), then the instruction pointer is incremented by the number of bytes specified by n, causing a branch. If A is non-zero, then no branch is taken, but the value in A is popped. J n is similar, except that it is unconditional.

LEND is designed to implement deterministic loops. It takes two parameters: in A there is a displacement which is to be subtracted from the instruction pointer should the instruction succeed; in the B register, there is a pointer to a two-word control block. Each time the instruction is executed, the value of the first word is incremented, and the second decremented. If the value remaining in the second word is greater than zero, the branch is taken, using the offset specified in the A register. Note that the value in A specifies how many bytes to go *back* by.

As an example, the Pascal code

```
FOR i := 3 TO 8 DO
   j := j + i;
```

would be implemented as

```
      LDC 3; STL block;
      LDC 8-3+1; STL block+1;
L1:   LDL j; LDL block; ADD; STL j;
      LDLP block;
      LDC L2-L1;
      LEND;
L2:
```

The two instructions J and LEND provide the points where the transputer may time-slice between low priority processes. Consequently, if a section of code does not make use of these two (for example, it uses CJ instead), then the process will never be time-sliced out, unless pre-empted by a high priority process.

3.3.2   Subroutine Calling

The remaining three instructions are designed to implement procedure calls.

CALL n	Call
RET	Return
GCALL	General Call

CALL n decrements the workspace pointer by four bytes, stores at the four words thus allocated (in descending order) the current contents of the C, B, A and instruction pointer registers and then increments the instruction pointer by the number of bytes specified by the operand n. It thus implements a relative call instruction. RET loads the instruction pointer with the value pointed to by the workspace pointer, and increments the workspace pointer by four words. Thus RET will always return from a CALL as long as the workspace pointer remains unchanged.

If this procedure call mechanism is found to be too restricting, a more general one may be implemented using GCALL, which just exchanges the contents of the A register and the instruction pointer. It is then up to the programmer to sort out such things as storing the return address and so on.

3.4 Process Scheduling and Control

3.4.1 Background

The transputer has built-in mechanisms to support the concurrent execution of processes. Processes may be operated at two levels of priority. Two queues of active processes are maintained, one for high, and one for low priority processes. A process can be in one of four states: executing; waiting to execute, which implies that it is in one of the active process queues; waiting for a timer event, which implies that it is in a timer queue, or waiting for a communication event, in which case it is in no queue.

A high priority process will execute without interruption until it terminates, or waits for a timer or communication event to take place. In this case, if there are any further high priority processes waiting to proceed then the process at the head of the high priority active process queue will be scheduled. If there are no high priority processes waiting to execute, then the next waiting low priority process will be scheduled. Low priority processes may be pre-empted at any time by a high priority process that becomes ready to execute. Low priority processes are time-sliced; if a low priority process executes a **Jump** or **Loop End** instruction, and has been executing for more than its time-slice period, it is descheduled and placed at the back of the low priority active queue, with the process at the head of the queue commencing execution.

3.4.2 Start Process and End Process

The transputer provides five instructions to allow the setting up of new processes, and the killing off of others. Two of the instructions are designed to directly support the occam view of concurrency, or more specifically, the occam **PAR** construct. In the occam program shown in figure 3.1, section P is executed first, and then (conceptually, at least), the current process is suspended, and three new processes are started which execute sections Q, R and S in parallel. Only when all three of these child processes have successfully terminated, is the parent process rescheduled, which then executes section T. If any of the children fail to terminate successfully, then the parent process will never be rescheduled.

The way that an occam compiler would treat the above code is in fact slightly different from that just described. Only two child processes would be set up, with the parent process taking over the execution of section S. The first two of the three processes to finish their section of

```
SEQ
  section P
  PAR
    section Q
    section R
    section S
  section T
```

Figure 3.1. An occam PAR construct.

code just terminate, while the last one to terminate resumes execution of section T.

The two instructions

STARTP	Start Process
ENDP	End Process

are designed specifically to implement this scheme. STARTP adds a new process to the back of the active process queue. It takes two parameters: the A register holds the address of the workspace that the new process will use, and B holds an offset in bytes from the current instruction (or more accurately, the next instruction) to the section of code that the new process is to execute. The new process is set at the same priority as the current process, and the current process continues execution with the next instruction. Note that the new execution address is specified relative to the old, following the usual transputer philosophy that code produced should be relocatable, unless the programmer tries very hard to do otherwise!

ENDP is designed to conditionally terminate a process. What it does is to decrement a count somewhere in memory. If this count is non-zero then it just terminates, that is to say, the next active process is taken from the queue and executed, and the current process is *not* added to the back of the queue. If on the other hand the count has reached zero, then the process continues, but at a different execution address, and with a different workspace pointer. More precisely, the instruction takes one parameter, an address in the A register. This address points to the workspace of the parent process. At location 0 in this workspace is the restart address of the parent process (in the example above this is the address of code section T). Location 1 holds the count of child processes. If the instruction decrements this value to zero, it sets its workspace pointer to the value in the A register, and its instruction

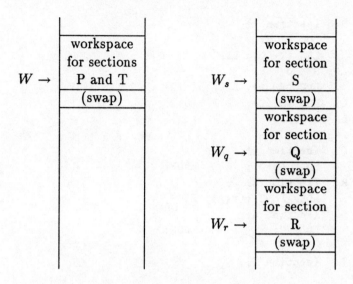

Figure 3.2. Workspaces for the PAR processes.

pointer to the value pointed to by A.

The PAR construct above would thus be executed as follows: the parent process, after having executed section P, stores the count three at local 1, and the address of the code for section T at local 0. It then executes two STARTP instructions, which set up processes to execute sections Q and R. It then performs a jump to section S.

At this point, there are three concurrent processes, executing sections Q, R and S. The first two of these processes to finish will terminate after decrementing the count. The last to terminate will then 'assume the role' of the parent process, executing section T.

Note that in occam, the compiler can determine at compile time the workspace requirements for each process. Thus it can allocate workspaces for Q and R at fixed positions below the workspace for the parent process. This is shown in figure 3.2. The figure on the left indicates the state of the workspace when there is only the single process running. The workspace pointer W points to the base of the workspace (i.e. location 0) of the process that executes section P and T.

A couple of words below the workspace are reserved for use by the scheduling hardware should the process be descheduled. (Note that this would be more, up to five words, if channel communication or timer ALTs are used by the process—see the next section for details.) The

```
P:   {section P}
     LDC 3; STL 1;
     LDC (T-L0); LDPI
L0:  STL 0;
     LDC (R-L1); LDLP -(q+2)-(r+2); STARTP;
L1:  LDC (Q-L2); LDLP -(q+2);         STARTP;
L2:  J (S-Q)

Q:   {section Q}
     LDLP (q+2);         ENDP;
R:   {section R}
     LDLP (q+2)+(r+2); ENDP;
S:   {section S}
     LDLP 0;            ENDP;

T:   {section T}
```

Figure 3.3. Code for a PAR construct.

second diagram shows the situation after the PAR section has been entered. The original process carrys on using the same workspace (which is assumed to be large enough to hold the local variables for P, T *and* S, while the two new processes are allocated new workspaces below the original.

Thus the code for the example above may be coded as in figure 3.3. Here, q and r are the sizes of workspace required for Q and R.

If it is not possible to determine at compile time the address of the original workspace relative to each of the children, then one possibility is that the address of the parent workspace be stored at the first location (say) of each of the child processes when they are being set up. Then the above code would be changed to look like that in figure 3.4.

Note that if any of the processes executing sections Q, R and S hang (for example if they execute Stop On Error after an error—see below), then no process will ever proceed to execute section T. Thus, if the section of occam program given above is itself part of a family of PAR processes, then that family's parent will eventually hang, and so on.

3.4.3   Other Process Instructions

There are three other instructions which initiate and terminate processes:

```
P:   {section P}
     LDC 3; STL 1;
     LDC (T-L0); LDPI
L0:  STL 0;
     LDLP 0;      STL  -(q+2)-(r+2);
     LDC (R-L1); LDLP -(q+2)-(r+2); STARTP;
     LDLP 0;      STL  -(q+2);
L1:  LDC (Q-L2); LDLP -(q+2);           STARTP;
L2:  J (S-Q)

Q:   {section Q}
     LDL 0; ENDP;
R:   {section R}
     LDL 0; ENDP;
S:   {section S}
     LDLP 0; ENDP;

T:   {section T}
```

Figure 3.4. Modified code for a PAR construct.

STOPP	Stop Process
STOPERR	Stop On Error
RUNP	Run Process

STOPP stops the current process. This means that the process's instruction pointer is stored at the first word below its workspace, and the next active waiting process is scheduled. Note that the current process is *not* added to the back of the active queue, so unless there is manual intervention by another process to reactivate it, the process is effectively dead. STOPERR does the same, but only if the error flag is set. Note the difference between these two instructions and ENDP, which terminates only if it is not the last of a family of processes, and assumes the role of the parent otherwise.

RUNP is the most general way of starting a new process. It takes one parameter, a process descriptor in the A register. A process descriptor is the address of the workspace for that process with the bottom bit set to the priority of that process (remember that since a workspace lies on a word boundary, the bottom few bits are not used). RUNP adds a new process to the back of the active queue specified by the priority bit. The new process will have the workspace as determined by the descriptor, and will begin execution at the address stored one word below that workspace.

So to start a new process with workspace W, entry point E and priority P,

```
LDC E; LDC W; STNL -1;
LDC W; LDC P; OR; RUNP;
```

would suffice. Note the contrast with STARTP, which starts a new process at the same priority as the current one, and whose execution address is specified relative to the current process.

RUNP is also ideally suited for restarting hung processes. A process that is waiting for a channel or timer event, or that has been stopped using STOPP or STOPERR always has its execution address stored at location −1 in its workspace. Thus, it can be restarted, as long as its workspace address and priority are known. In the case of channel communication (see next section), the process descriptor of the waiting process is stored in the channel word.

3.4.4   Process Register Manipulation

There are four registers associated with the active process queues that may be directly accessed by the programmer (with caution). These are the front and back, high and low priority active queue registers. The instructions

STHF   Store High Priority Front Pointer
STHB   Store High Priority Back Pointer
STLF   Store Low Priority Front Pointer
STLB   Store Low Priority Back Pointer

store the value in the A register in the relevant register. On booting, it is necessary to store *MinInt* in the high and low priority front registers before any process scheduling takes place; the back pointers do not need to be initialised. It hardly needs to be stated that these instructions are highly dangerous, especially as link hardware may modify the active queues even while a high priority process is running.

The instructions

SAVEH   Save High Priority Queue Registers
SAVEL   Save Low Priority Queue Registers

store the contents of the front and back pointers in two successive words pointed to by the A register (the front one first). Finally,

LDPRI   Load Priority

loads a value (0 or 1) into A representing the priority of the current process.

3.5   Inter-process Communication

3.5.1   Channels

Inter-process communication and synchronisation are carried out using channels. A channel is an abstract connection between exactly two processes. One process sends a stream of bytes down the channel to another process, which reads them in and stores them. If a process tries to send or receive data through a channel when the other process is not ready, then it will be descheduled until that other process becomes ready, thus achieving synchronisation.

For two processes running on the same transputer, a channel is implemented by using a word somewhere in memory that is shared between the two processes. This word is referred to as the channel word. Before any communication can take place, this word must be initialised to the value *MinInt* (minimum integer), which with the transputer's signed address space, is interpreted as the lowest address in memory. This is significant, because this value can never be the address of a valid workspace. The channel word would normally be initialised by the parent process of the two communicating children, to ensure that it is initialised before either of them attempt to communicate. When a process attempts to communicate, it examines the contents of the channel word; if the value is *MinInt*, then the other process is not ready, so it stores its process descriptor in the channel word, and deschedules. When the other process is ready, it examines the channel word and finds a valid process descriptor. It thus knows that the other process is ready, and so transfers the block of bytes, and restarts the other process.

If a process deschedules while waiting for channel input or output, it stores its instruction pointer at location −1 in its local workspace, and the address of the data to be transferred from or to at location −3. This last item of data is required in order for the second process to be able to implement the data transfer.

The important thing to realise is that all this is implemented within the microcode of the transputer; at the machine code level, a process just executes an instruction requesting that data be read from or written to a channel.

For two processes running on separate transputers, the two machines must be connected by a hardware INMOS link in order for them to directly communicate. In this case, communication via a channel is taken care of by hardware within the transputer. When a process makes a request to send data out through a channel to another transputer, that process is descheduled. Hardware determines when the other transputer is ready, and then transfers the data using direct memory access (DMA). When all the data has been transferred, the process is rescheduled. While all this is happening, other processes may be executed.

At the machine code level, hardware links appear identical to internal channels, and the same instructions are used for both. The only thing that distinguishes between them, is that for external communication, the address of the channel word passed as a parameter to an input or output instruction is specified as one of the first few locations in memory. The microcode of the instructions detect that the address is one of the special reserved locations and pass their parameters on to the link hardware for the link associated with that address.

3.5.2   Input and Output

The instructions

OUT	Output Message
OUTWORD	Output Word
OUTBYTE	Output Byte
IN	Input Message

deal with channel input and output. The OUT instruction takes three parameters: A holds the number of bytes to transfer, B points to the channel word to be used for the communication, and C points to the start of the data to be sent out through the channel. OUTWORD and OUTBYTE are similar, except that they transfer a single word or byte contained in the A register. They also have the side effect of overwriting location 0 in the local workspace. IN performs the opposite of OUT by reading in a sequence of bytes. All these instructions reset the channel word to *MinInt* after a successful transfer, ready for the next communication.

A quirk of the transputer is that although both the inputting and outputting processes specify the length of the message being sent, the quantity of data actually transferred is determined by the length specified by the second of the two processes to become ready. No check is performed to see that the two lengths have the same value. For communication over external links, the quantity of data sent out and received

```
PRI ALT
  chan ? data
    process(data)
  flag & timer ? AFTER n
    timeout := TRUE
  NOT flag & SKIP
    nodata := TRUE
```

Figure 3.5. ALT example.

is determined respectively by the output and input processes on the two transputers. It is up to the programmer to ensure that the lengths are specified the same on both processors. If the receiving process requests more data than is sent, then it will hang, pending further data being sent, and vice versa.

Strangely enough, there are no corresponding INWORD and INBYTE instructions, although there does not appear to be any reason for excluding them.

There is one further instruction of direct relevance to channels, and this is

RESETCH   Reset Channel

which sets an internal channel word to *MinInt*, or resets the link hardware for an external channel. This instruction should not need to be used during normal programming, since channels are automatically reinitialised after communication. It is designed for use in fault-tolerant situations where communications may break down halfway through a transfer.

3.5.3 Alternatives

The problem with the above instructions is that they commit a process to a particular communication, and will cause it to hang indefinitely if the other process never becomes ready to communicate. The transputer has a suite of instructions, collectively referred to as ALT instructions, which allow one of a series of events to be chosen. The chosen event is the one that occurs first. These instructions are optimised to support the occam ALT construct, of which a brief résumé will now be given.

A typical example of an ALT construct is shown in figure 3.5. In fact, this example uses a 'priority ALT', which simply guarantees that if two events occur simultaneously, the one listed earlier in the construct is chosen.

This ALT consists of three 'guards', together with the code that they are guarding. The first guard, chan ? data, says that if the first event to occur is data appearing on channel *chan*, then read it into the variable *data*, and process it. The second guard demonstrates an optional boolean flag that can be associated with a guard, separated from it by an ampersand (&). In this case, the guard is processed only if the flag is *true*. This second guard demonstrates a timer input, which is basically an event that occurs when the current time is after the time specified by the value *n*. (Confusingly, the occam syntax for timers is the same as that for channels.) The final guard, a SKIP, is one that always succeeds.

If the event takes place for a particular guard, that guard is said to have *fired*. A guard may have already fired when the ALT construct is entered (for example, a ready channel, a time in the past, or a SKIP guard), or it may fire at some point in the future, (for example, a channel that becomes ready to communicate, or a time that is reached), or it may never fire (boolean part of guard evaluates to *false*). If more than one guard has fired, or fires, simultaneously, then the one first in the PRI ALT construct is chosen (for an ordinary ALT it is random; it simply depends upon the order in which the compiler plants the Disable instructions—see page 47).

The overall effect of the example can be described as follows. The construct can be entered with *flag* set to either *true* or *false*. If the construct is entered with *flag* set to *true*, then an attempt is made to input some data from the channel *chan*. If however, this does not occur within a specified time interval, then the variable *timeout* is set instead.

On the other hand, if *flag* is set to *false*, then the channel *chan* is checked to see if it has data already. If so, it is read in and processed, otherwise the flag *nodata* is set.

It is important to realise that the ALT provides a passive wait; that is to say, if no guards have fired, the process is descheduled, and other processing may continue until a guard fires. Note also that an ALT may have an arbitrary number of channel, timer and skip guards.

3.5.4   ALT Structure

The way ALTs are implemented can be described as follows. The first thing that is done is to *start* the ALT by setting some flags to indicate that an ALT sequence is taking place. Then the various guards must be *enabled*; this is the process of checking channel words used by the guards to see if there are any processes ready to communicate, finding the earliest time that a timer guard is waiting for, seeing if a guard has already fired, and so on. Following this is the *wait*, which is where the process goes to sleep until such time as a guard fires. Next, each guard is *disabled*: this is the process of determining which of the guards has fired. Finally, the ALT is *ended* by jumping to the section of code associated with the guard that fired.

The words within italics are the names that INMOS have given to the various parts of an ALT sequence of instructions, and the name of each individual instruction is closely related to this.

3.5.5 ALT Instructions

The two instructions for starting an ALT sequence are

> ALT   Alt Start
> TALT   Timer Alt Start

Both these instructions set the word at location −3 in the workspace to the value *MinInt*+1. This value is used to indicate 'no guards have fired yet'. The choice of this location and value is important, because it corresponds to the data address stored by an IN or OUT instruction when it deschedules. This means that a process executing an OUT instruction on a channel shared with the ALT process will be able to tell that the process it is communicating with is an ALT process, rather than just an IN. This is because *MinInt*+1 can never be a valid data address.

In addition, TALT sets location −4 to *MinInt*+2, an arbitrary-valued flag indicating that 'no valid time has yet been stored'. TALT should only be used for ALT constructs which have at least one timer guard, since it uses a further two locations below the workspace, compared with ALT.

> ENBC   Enable Channel
> ENBS   Enable Skip
> ENBT   Enable Timer

These three instructions perform the enabling discussed above. One of these instructions is executed for each guard in the ALT construct. Their parameters consist of a boolean value, which corresponds to the boolean part of the guard, discussed above. In addition, ENBC and ENBT have an extra parameter, respectively an address of a channel word, and a value indicating a time. The effect of these instructions is to do nothing if the boolean has the value *false*. If on the other hand it is *true*, then the effects are as follows.

ENBS sets the flag at location -3 to $MinInt+3$, indicating that a guard has fired. ENBT stores the time value at location -5 if it is an earlier time than any previously recorded. In doing this, it makes use of the flag at location -4, which indicates whether a time has yet been recorded. Finally, ENBC examines the channel word. If the channel word contains the value $MinInt$, indicating that the other process is not waiting on the channel, then it stores its process descriptor in the channel word, in the same way that a normal communicating process would. If, on the other hand, the channel word does not contain the value $MinInt$, then there are two possibilities. Either there is a process waiting at the other end of the channel, or a previous guard of the ALT process is waiting on the same channel. Note that it is legal, although unusual, for two guards to wait on the same channel. The way of telling these two cases apart is that if the process descriptor stored in the channel word differs from that of the ALT process, then there is another process waiting on the channel. If this is the case, then location -3 is set to $MinInt+3$, indicating that a guard has fired.

One important difference between an ALT channel input, and normal channel input must be mentioned here. The code that implements the ALT never actually transfers data across a channel. All it does is detect whether a channel has become ready, and passes control on to the section of code that deals with that channel. Thus the first instruction in a section of code following a channel guard would normally be an IN instruction. This has important implications on the design of the OUT instruction. Normally, if an OUT instruction is executed and its channel word does not contain $MinInt$, it assumes that the other process is ready, copies the block of data, and reschedules the other process. If however, that other process is an ALT process, it must refrain from doing this. Instead, it must pretend to be the first of the two processes to become ready by storing its process descriptor in the channel word; it must then reschedule the ALT if appropriate. It can base all its decisions on the contents of location -3 in the ALTs workspace.

The next two instructions perform the actual wait during an ALT:

ALTWT   Alt Wait
TALTWT   Timer Alt Wait.

One of these two instructions should be executed after all the enable instructions. Their effect is to deschedule the ALT process if location −3 contains *MinInt*+1, i.e. if no guards have fired. If the ALT is descheduled, it will be reawakened when a communicating process becomes ready or, in the case of TALTWT, it may also reawaken if the time to wait until, comes to pass. TALTWT must be used instead of ALTWT if any of the guards wait on a time. As well as examining location −3, it checks to see if locations −4 and −5 indicate a valid time; if this time is in the future, then the ALT is added to the timer queue and descheduled. If an ALT process is descheduled, ALTWT and TALTWT set location −3 to the value *MinInt*+2, to indicate this fact to the process at the other end of any of the channels. If an ALT process is subsequently reactivated, then this location will be set to *MinInt*+3, indicating that a guard has finally fired.

One final action of these two instructions is to set a flag at location 0 in the workspace to the value −1.

Next come the disable instructions.

DISC	Disable Channel
DISS	Disable Skip
DIST	Disable Timer

One of these instructions must be executed for each guard in the ALT construct. Each instruction has a parameter specifying the value of the boolean flag in the guard. If this flag is *false*, the instruction is ignored. These boolean values *must* have the same values as in their corresponding Enable instructions. The occam compiler simply calculates the set of boolean expressions in the guards twice. Since occam does not allow shared variables, the results will always have the same value. An alternative approach (and one that seems a lot more efficient), is to evaluate the booleans once, storing the results in an array somewhere for use by the Disable instructions.

The second parameter common to all three Disable instructions is an offset, which gives the location of the code to be executed for that particular guard, relative to the Alt End instruction (see page 48). DISC and DIST each have one further parameter; a pointer to the channel word, or the time that was to be waited until. The comments above regarding evaluation of the boolean flags apply equally to the timer values.

The effect of these instructions is to determine whether that particular guard has fired, and if so to store the offset at location 0. This location is initialised to –1 by ALTWT; a Disable instruction will only store its offset there if the value is still –1. This establishes the order of priority if multiple guards have fired. Thus in an occam PRI ALT, the Disable instructions are planted in the same order that the guards appear in the construct, whereas the compiler is free to reorder the disabling for an ordinary ALT. A channel guard is deemed to have fired if its channel word holds a valid process descriptor and that descriptor is different from the ALT's descriptor; a timer guard has fired if its time value is before the current time; and a skip guard is always deemed to have fired. DISC and DIST also 'disable' a channel or timer if the ALT has not fired on that particular channel or timer. For a channel, if the channel word contains the process descriptor of the ALT process, then this value is reset to *MinInt*; for the timer, it removes the ALT process from the current priority timer queue if its time has still to come to pass. It is important that they are 'disabled'; after the ALTWT or TALTWT instruction has been executed, location –3 will contain *MinInt*+3. This value is used by the OUT instruction and the timer hardware to recognise an ALT that has already fired on another guard, and thus to not take the normal action. However, once the ALTEND instruction has been reached, location –3 can no longer be guaranteed to hold a valid value, so any remaining channels or timers must be made inactive.

The last remaining instruction is

> ALTEND   Alt End

which performs a relative jump based on the contents of location 0.

Finally, the code shown in figure 3.6 implements the ALT construct which was described at the beginning of the section in figure 3.5 (page 43).

3.6   Miscellaneous

There are a few remaining transputer instructions which perform miscellaneous tasks.

3.6.1   Timers

The transputer provides three instructions for dealing with the hardware timers.

```
    TALT;
    LDLP chan; LDC true; ENBC;
    LDC  n;    LDL flag; ENBT;
    LDL flag;  EQC 0;    ENBS;
    TALTWT;
    LDLP chan; LDC true; LDC (A-A); DISC;
    LDC  n;    LDL flag; LDC (B-A); DIST;
    LDL  flag; EQC 0;    LDC (C-A); DISS;
    ALTEND;
 A: LDLP data; LDLP chan; LDC 1; BCNT; IN;
    --call process(data)
    J (Z-B);
 B: LDC true;
    STL timeout;
    J (Z-C);
 C: LDC true;
    STL nodata;
 Z: --etc
```

Figure 3.6. Code to implement a timer ALT.

STTIMER	Store Timer
LDTIMER	Load Timer
TIN	Timer Input

STTIMER sets the values of the low and high priority timer registers to the value in the A register. LDTIMER pushes the value of the current priority timer register into the A register. Finally, TIN suspends the current process until the time in the current priority timer register is after the value specified in the A register; note that this is a passive wait, and other processes may execute in the meantime. This instruction works by inserting the current process into a sorted linked list of processes waiting for a time. Each time the timer is incremented, it is checked against the process at the head of the queue, and if necessary, that process is reactivated.

3.6.2 Flags

Finally, there are a set of instructions for manipulating various transputer flags.

SETERR	Set Error
TESTERR	Test Error False and Clear

The transputer's error flag is normally set when an arithmetic or checking instruction finds something at fault. SETERR is a way of deliberately setting this flag. TESTERR on the other hand, sets the A register to *false* if the error flag is set. It also clears the flag for further use. Note that the error flag is 'sticky', that is to say, it will not be cleared by a subsequent arithmetic operation that does not overflow. This instruction is usually followed by a Conditional Jump, which jumps if A is *false*. The status of the error flag is preserved when a low priority process is interrupted by a high priority one, but not when a process is descheduled normally (e.g. during channel communication, or timeslicing following a J or LEND instruction).

The transputer has a halt-on-error flag which, if set, causes the transputer to halt the next time the error flag gets set. Note that it is the whole transputer, not just the process that gets halted! The following instructions

CLRHALTERR	Clear Halt-On-Error Flag
SETHALTERR	Set Halt-On-Error Flag
TESTHALTERR	Test Halt-On-Error Flag

allow the flag to be cleared, set, and its current value to be read (by putting it in the A register). Finally,

TESTPRANAL	Test Processor Analysing

loads *true* or *false* into the A register depending on whether the *analyse* pin was set on the transputer the last time it received a hardware reset. This instruction is commonly used to allow bootstrap code to determine whether to run ordinary or diagnostic code.

Chapter 4

Example Programs

4.1 Introduction

The purpose of this chapter is to illustrate with examples some of the instructions and ideas which you have met in the previous chapters. Most of the examples require a basic knowledge of occam, and so will be of most benefit to those readers familiar with this language.

Why should we use assembly language? Occam is one of the languages used to program transputers and INMOS quite rightly maintains that compiled occam can only be marginally improved on by the very best assembly language writer. The usual reasons given for the use of assembly language is to manage memory efficiently and to communicate with peripherals but occam has features already built-in to enable the user to do this. What the designers of occam and the transputer have not done is to allow the user to manipulate the in-built scheduling and communication mechanisms of the transputer in occam. Thus most of the examples in this chapter are concerned with these features. The exceptions to this are the first few examples which have been included to introduce some of the terminology.

There are a number of transputer assemblers available commercially or in the public domain. All of the examples in this chapter were originally assembled using an assembler developed in the Computer Science department at the University of Sheffield. The difficulty is that each assembler has different pseudo opcodes and facilities. To appeal to as large an audience as possible, the examples have been recoded using the occam 'GUY' construct, which enables in-line assembly language to be used within occam. All of the examples have been developed on a T800

```
#USE userio
BOOL BO:
INT VO, Any:
SEQ
  GUY
    LDC 8000          -- #8000012A  ldc 8000
    STL VO            -- #8000012E  stl 2
    LDC TRUE          -- #8000012F  ldc 1
    STL BO            -- #80000130  stl 3
  write.int(screen, VO, 0)
  IF
    BO = TRUE
      write.full.string(screen, "  TRUE")
    BO = FALSE
      write.full.string(screen, "  FALSE")
  keyboard ? Any
```

Figure 4.1. Constant/Boolean example.

using occam and the debugger available in the INMOS Transputer Development System (TDS). They could just as easily have been produced using the INMOS standalone toolset. Even if you do not use occam, or if you have your own assembler, you should find these examples informative and easy to understand.

In each of the occam programs the input/output library *userio* has been used. This library is supplied with the TDS system, and as it should be obvious from the process names and parameters what these processes do, their details are omitted for compactness.

4.2   Introductory Examples

The GUY construct within occam is very useful and it has a number of attractive features; but it has some limitations and also some peculiar effects. Thus a number of trivial examples are included in this section to familiarise the reader with the notation and to point out some of the peculiarities of GUY.

One method of debugging programs is to put a SETERR instruction at an appropriate point in a program. The program is then compiled, linked and run. When the SETERR instruction is executed, this sets the error pin on the transputer and the INMOS debugger [3] can then

```
PROC Add( VAL INT Num1, Num2, INT Result)
  GUY
    LDL   Num1        -- #80000104  ldl  1
    LDL   Num2        -- #80000105  ldl  2
    ADD               -- #80000106  add
    STL   Result      -- #80000108  ldl  3
                      -- #80000109  stnl 0
  :                   -- #8000010A  ret
#USE userio
INT Num1, Num2, Result, Ch, Any:
SEQ
  Ch := 0
  write.full.string(screen, "Input first number ")
  read.echo.int(keyboard, screen, Num1, Ch)
  write.full.string(screen,"*c*nInput second number ")
  read.echo.int(keyboard, screen, Num2, Ch)
  Add (Num1, Num2, Result)
  write.full.string(screen,"*c*nThe sum of these is ")
  write.int(screen, Result,0)
  keyboard ? Any
```

Figure 4.2. ADD example.

be used to inspect the code. Using this procedure on a simple program brings to light the first inconsistency in the system. Inside the GUY construct the transputer instructions must be in capital letters, but the disassembler displays them in lower case letters. This is a trivial difference, but it is indicative that others may follow.

The example in figure 4.1 shows some of the nice features of GUY. Constants (e.g. 8000 and TRUE) can be input in a user friendly way, and the disassembled code produced by the debugger matches the original GUY code. It should be noted however, that the instruction LDC 8000 does in fact consist of five instructions, four Prefix instructions and one Load Constant instruction. GUY handles all positive and negative prefixing automatically; this includes the addressing of data within the workspace, as well as constants. TRUE and FALSE are automatically replaced by 1 and 0 respectively. Another nice feature of GUY is that occam variables which are in scope can be referred to by name within the GUY construct. Unfortunately the disassembler does not reproduce the symbolic names used in the original GUY.

The disassembled code obtained from the debugger has been included

```
PROC ArrayTest (BYTE a, INT b, []BYTE NonLocalArray1,
           [5]INT NonLocalArray2, INT c)
  [512]INT Array:
  SEQ
    Array[511] := INT('3')
    SEQ
      a:= NonLocalArray1[(SIZE NonLocalArray1)-1]
      b:= NonLocalArray2[(SIZE NonLocalArray2)-1]
      c:= Array[(SIZE Array)-1]
  :
#USE userio
[510]BYTE Array1:
[5]INT Array2:
BYTE a:
INT b, c, Any:
SEQ
  Array1[509] := '1'
  Array2[4] := INT('2')
  ArrayTest (a, b, Array1, Array2, c)
  write.int(screen, INT a, 10)
  write.int(screen, b, 10)
  write.int(screen, c, 10)
  keyboard ? Any
```

Figure 4.3. occam version of array example.

in the occam program as comments. A comment in occam starts with
'--'. This is done where appropriate to emphasise the differences between the GUY input and the disassembled output or to show more
clearly the code which has been created by the compiler. It is possible that your system may give different addresses, but they should only
be displaced by a constant from those shown. The disassembled code
shows that the variables in the local workspace are placed in reverse
order, hence *Any* is at location 1, *V0* at location 2 and *B0* at location
3. Note also that BOOLs and BYTEs occupy one word in the workspace,
that is 32 bits for T4s and T8s.

The second example, given in figure 4.2, illustrates that in some cases
the disassembled code produced by the debugger differs from the original
GUY code. The reasons for this will become clear as we examine the
code. Two of the parameters to the procedure *Add* are value parameters,
namely *Num1* and *Num2*. The values of these parameters are placed
at locations 1 and 2 of the workspace. However, the third parameter,

518	*c*
517	Address of *NonLocalArray2*
516	Size of _____ *NonLocalArray1*
515	Address of *NonLocalArray1*
514	*b*
513	*a*
512	Return Address
⋮	⋮
0	*Array*

Figure 4.4. Diagram of the workspace for *TestArray*.

namely *Result* is a call by reference parameter, and a pointer to the actual location of *Result* is placed at location 3 of the workspace. Note that the parameters of the procedure appear in the workspace in the same order as they do in the specification of the procedure, whereas the local variables, if there are any, appear in reverse order.

Accessing parameters or variables using GUY is done by LDL or STL irrespective of the fact that the parameter or variable may be local or non-local, or called by reference or value. The compiler has enough information from the surrounding occam to produce the required transputer instructions. The disassembled code produced by the debugger is the exact code required by the transputer apart from negative and positive prefixes. If you are using your own assembler you may have to translate some of the GUY instructions to more literal equivalents. For instance, the STL Result may have to be replaced by LDL Result; STNL 0. Note also that the compiler plants the RET, whereas most assemblers would expect you to type it in.

The last example in this section is contained in figures 4.3, 4.4 and 4.5, and it demonstrates some more of the features of GUY. Figure 4.3 is a purely occam program and figure 4.5 shows how the procedure *ArrayTest* in figure 4.3 could be coded using GUY. The procedure *ArrayTest* returns in *a*, *b* and *c* the last values of the arrays *Array*, *NonLocalArray1* and *NonLocalArray2* respectively. The main purpose of this example is to show how arrays are accessed and passed as parameters. In addition, the example shows how to use the SIZE operator within GUY.

The workspace for *ArrayTest* is shown in figure 4.4. Variable sized arrays such as *NonLocalArray1* have a pointer to the start of the array,

```
PROC ArrayTest (BYTE a, INT b, []BYTE NonLocalArray1,
         [5]INT NonLocalArray2, INT c)
  [512]INT Array:                  -- #80000AF8 ajw -512
  SEQ
    Array[511] := INT('3')         -- #80000AFB ldc 51
                                   -- #80000AFD stl 511
    GUY
      -- a:= NonLocalArray1[(SIZE NonLocalArray1)-1]
      LDL  SIZE (NonLocalArray1)   -- #80000B00 ldl  516
      ADC  -1                      -- #80000B03 adc  -1
      LDL  SIZE (NonLocalArray1)   -- #80000B05 ldl  516
      CSUB0                        -- #80000B08 csub0
      LDLP NonLocalArray1          -- #80000B0A ldl  515
      BSUB                         -- #80000B0D bsub
      LB                           -- #80000B0E lb
      STL  a                       -- #80000B0F ldl  513
                                   -- #80000B12 stnl 0
      -- b:= NonLocalArray2[(SIZE NonLocalArray2)-1]
      LDLP  NonLocalArray2         -- #80000B13 ldl  517
      LDNL ((SIZE NonLocalArray2) -1)
                                   -- #80000B16 ldnl 4
      STL  b                       -- #80000B17 ldl  514
                                   -- #80000B1A stnl 0
      -- c:= Array[(SIZE Array)-1]
      LDLP  Array                  -- #80000B1B ldlp 0
      LDNL  ((SIZE Array) -1)      -- #80000B1C ldnl 511
      STL  c                       -- #80000B1F ldl  518
                                   -- #80000B22 stnl 0
    :                              -- #80000B23 ajw  512
                                   -- #80000B26 ret
```

Figure 4.5. GUY code to replace the *ArrayTest* procedure.

and a constant indicating the size of the array placed at the appropriate
places in the workspace. This is necessary, as it is only at run time
that both of these pieces of information will be known. Conversely only
a pointer to the fixed sized array *NonLocalArray2* is required, as the
compiler knows the exact size of the array at compile time. Arrays
in occam are indexed from 0, with the zero element occupying a lower
location in the workspace than the last element.

If local variables are declared within a procedure, then they can
be accessed from within the GUY construct. The appropriate AJW
instructions are planted by the compiler at the start of the procedure,

and also at the end of the procedure, prior to the RET instruction. The local variables and parameters are then all positive offsets from the workspace pointer. The local variables appear first in the workspace (in the reverse order to their declaration), followed by the address of the next instruction of the calling procedure, followed lastly by the parameters in the order they are declared (see figure 4.4).

The SIZE operator is treated in two different ways in GUY. If it is used to size a local array, such as *Array*, or a fixed sized array passed as a parameter, such as *NonLocalArray2*, it returns the size of the array. However, if it is used to size a variable sized array passed as a parameter, such as *NonLocalArray1*, it returns the location in the workspace which will contain the size of the array when the procedure is called.

In GUY, if the instruction LDLP is used in conjunction with a local variable, such as *Array*, a pointer to the appropriate workspace element is loaded. However, if LDLP is used in conjunction with a parameter which has been passed as a pointer, such as *NonLocalArray1*, then GUY converts this to a LDL instruction for the appropriate workspace location. Suppose LDL NonLocalArray1 had been used instead of LDLP, then GUY would have converted this to LDL 515, LDNL 0, which is completely wrong in this context.

The GUY instructions prior to and including the CSUB0 instruction illustrate how the compiler range-checks array accesses prior to loading. The GUY code for range-checking is not strictly necessary, as the programmer knows in advance that he is accessing a valid array element (i.e. the last element), but it shows the general approach, and would be necessary if it were the fifth from last element being accessed, for example. If the first element of the array had been required, the range-checking code would have been replaced by LDL 0, LDL SIZE NonLocalArray1, CSUB0. Accesses to fixed-sized arrays by constant indices can be performed without range-checking code; this is because the compiler can perform the range-checking at compile time, or the GUY programmer can manually check his or her own code. However, range-checking must be carried out at run time for variable-sized arrays, or fixed-sized arrays with variable indices.

To use GUY within occam procedures, the programmer must know how parameters are passed by the compiler. In the product version of the occam compiler, the values of all value parameters which are 32 bits or less are placed in the appropriate places in the workspace, and all other value parameters are passed as pointers. Thus VAL INT64 and VAL REAL64 are passed as pointers; it is then up to the compiler or the

GUY writer to make sure that these parameters are only accessed by value. All other parameters are passed by reference. That is, a pointer to the parameter is placed in the workspace at the appropriate point. The length of a variable sized array parameter is placed in the workspace in the location immediately above the pointer to the array.

4.3   Communication Examples

This section contains a number of examples concerned with input and output. The first two examples illustrate how we investigated the operation of some of the transputer instructions. *The Compiler Writer's Guide* [4] produced by INMOS, although useful, assumes that the exact operation of some instructions, such as ALTWT and OUT, are irrelevant. We feel that a fuller description is both educational and may be of use if someone has an unusual use of the instruction.

The third example combines the use of the input and output instructions in a single buffer procedure, showing that GUY procedures can still use protocols for channel communication. In addition, this example demonstrates a bug in the product release of the occam/GUY compiler.

Finally, the last example in this section shows how several processes can share the same channel, breaking the normal occam rules which state that only two processes may share a particular channel. This demonstrates that GUY procedures can be used to violate the normal occam conventions if this is required.

4.3.1   Programs to Inspect Workspace Usage

During the writing of this book, it was useful to take snapshots of the current workspace usage after the execution of particular instructions. The examples given in figures 4.6 and 4.7 show how this was done. In figure 4.6 we are checking the operation of the IN instruction, but we could have easily replaced the instructions between the two dashed lines with other experimental code, as we have done in figure 4.7.

The operation of these programs will now be described. In both examples, the program works by executing some code with its workspace pointer set to point to a locally declared array *Wspace*. In this way it is possible to examine the contents of the workspace after a particular instruction, or sequence of instructions has been executed. In fact, we

```
#USE userio

PROC TestInst(CHAN OF ANY In, []INT wspace)
  GUY
    LDL   1 -- load pointer to channel word
    LDC   5 -- load offset into array
    LDL   2 -- load pointer to start of array
    WSUB    -- calculate new workspace pointer
    GAJW    -- transfer to new workspace
    STL   1 -- save old workspace pointer
    STL   2 -- save pointer to channel word
    ---------------------------------------------------------
    LDLP  3 -- get pointer to buffer location
    LDL   2 -- load pointer to channel word
    LDC   4 -- transfer 4 bytes
    IN
    ---------------------------------------------------------
    LDL   1 -- load old workspace pointer
    GAJW    -- return to old workspace
  :

VAL MaxSize IS 10:
[MaxSize]INT Wspace:
CHAN OF ANY ToTestInst:
INT Any:
SEQ
  SEQ i=0 FOR MaxSize          -- initialize wspace
    Wspace[i]:=0
  PAR
****  ToTestInst ! 8
****  TestInst (ToTestInst, Wspace)
  SEQ
    SEQ i=0 FOR MaxSize         -- print out Wspace
      SEQ
        write.full.string (screen, "*c*nLoc ")
        write.int (screen, i-5, 0)
        write.full.string (screen, ": ")
        write.hex.int(screen, Wspace[i], 8)
    keyboard ! Any
```

Figure 4.6. Program to inspect workspace after IN instruction.

```
#USE userio
PROC TestInst(CHAN OF ANY In, []INT wspace)
  GUY
    LDL   1  -- load pointer to channel word
    LDC   5  -- load offset into array
    LDL   2  -- load pointer to start of array
    WSUB     -- calculate new workspace pointer
    GAJW     -- transfer to new workspace
    STL   1  -- save old workspace pointer
    STL   2  -- save pointer to channel word
    -----------------------------------------------------
    ALT      -- test workspace usage of ALT
    ALTWT    -- followed by ALTWT
    -----------------------------------------------------
    LDL   1  -- load old workspace pointer
    GAJW     -- return to old workspace
  :

VAL MaxSize IS 10:
CHAN OF ANY ToTestInst:
[MaxSize]INT Wspace:
INT Any:
SEQ
  SEQ i=0 FOR MaxSize       -- initialize Wspace
    Wspace[i]:=0
  PAR
    TestInst (ToTestInst, Wspace)
    SEQ                     -- make sure other
      keyboard ! Any        -- process has descheduled
      SEQ i=0 FOR MaxSize   -- print Wspace
        SEQ
          write.full.string (screen, "*c*nLoc ")
          write.int (screen, i-5, 0)
          write.full.string (screen, ": ")
          write.hex.int(screen, Wspace[i], 8)
      keyboard ! Any
      GUY                       -- restart descheduled TestInst
        LDLP Wspace             -- get pointer to start of
        LDNLP 5                 -- workspace for TestInst
        LDC   1                 -- make this a low priority
        OR                      -- descriptor
        RUNP
```

Figure 4.7. Program to inspect workspace after an ALTWT instruction.

offset from W	1st run	2nd run
4	#00000000	#00000000
3	#00000008	#00000008
2	#800000F0	#800000F0
1	#800000C4	#800000D4
0	#00000000	#00000000
−1	#00000000	#80000168
−2	#00000000	#00000000
−3	#00000000	#80000114
−4	#00000000	#00000000
−5	#00000000	#00000000

Figure 4.8. Example output from two runs of the program shown in figure 4.6

set the workspace pointer to point to *Wspace*[5], so that the five locations below the workspace pointer can be examined.

The first action of the program is to initialise the workspace *Wspace* to known values, usually zero. Then the procedure *TestInst*, which includes the instructions under investigation, is called. The **GAJW** instruction exchanges the contents of the A register, which should contain the new workspace pointer, with the current contents of the workspace pointer. Any extra information required can be stored in the workspace for use either in the procedure and/or to be displayed later.

In this example the address of the channel word *In* is required after the workspace has been changed. Thus it is passed on the evaluation stack and stored in a convenient place in the new workspace, as is the value of the old workspace pointer. Having done a **GAJW**, the variables in the old workspace could have been accessed by **LDL 1, LDNL x**, where **x** is the required offset.

In the previous GUY examples, variables and parameters in the workspace can be accessed by name, but GUY can also access variables by their position. In this mode it is up to the programmer to keep track of the workspace usage. Note also that in this direct mode, the programmer must remember if a location contains a pointer or data, and these must be dealt with appropriately.

When run, the *TestInst* procedure either terminates naturally, as in figure 4.6, or it is descheduled waiting for input/output, as in figure 4.7. In the second case, extra GUY instructions have to be added into another process to restart the *TestInst* process. Finally, the *TestInst* procedure uses the previously stored old workspace pointer and another GAJW to restore the old workspace.

In figure 4.7, the *TestInst* process will be descheduled by the ALTWT instruction. When a process is descheduled, it saves a pointer to the next instruction at the location immediately below the workspace pointer. In this particular case, a pointer to the instruction LDL 1 is stored at *Wspace*[4]. The only other process which can proceed is the second process within the PAR. This second process waits for a keypress: this ensures that the other process has actually descheduled, no matter the order of the processes; then it writes out the contents of the workspace. Finally, an external GUY construct is used to restart the descheduled process. If this is not done, the system will deadlock as one of the processes within the PAR has not terminated.

This example shows how to use the RUNP instruction, which expects the process descriptor of the new process to be in the A register when it is called, and the address of where it has to start execution to have been stored at the location below the workspace. Remember that the instruction pointer was stored at the desired location when the *TestInst* process was descheduled while executing the ALTWT.

The findings of the investigation of the IN instructions will be given now, but the findings of the ALT instructions will be dealt with in section 4.4, where a complete example is given of the use of the ALT instructions.

Note that use of the workspace above location 0 is made by the assembly language process, whereas use of the space below location 0 is made by the microcode of the IN instruction. The left column of figure 4.8 shows the contents of the workspace for the program in figure 4.6 with the instructions inside the PAR in the order given. The right-hand column in figure 4.8 shows the workspace usage with the two starred instructions reversed. The left-hand column shows that the process ToTestChan ! 8 was executed first, transferring control to the *TestInst* process, which does not deschedule on reaching the IN instruction, as it is the second process. It then transfers the four bytes and reschedules the other process. In this case, the *TestInst* process makes no use of the locations below the workspace. In the second run with the starred instructions reversed, the *TestInst* process is executed first. In this case, when the IN instruction is executed, it stores the instruction pointer at location −1 and it stores a pointer to the message at location −3 of the workspace. In both cases, after the execution of *TestInst*, the workspace contains the old workspace pointer, a pointer to the channel word and the data transferred at locations 1, 2, and 3 respectively. The workspace pointers are different because the order of the compilation has been reversed.

In general, when inputting or outputting, the first process to start the communication is descheduled, the instruction pointer is stored at location −1 and a pointer to the message to be transferred is stored at location −3 of the workspace. Note that the number of bytes to be transferred is not stored. In an occam program this is not necessary as the compiler will have checked that the inputting and outputting processes wish to transfer the same number of bytes. Thus when the second process is scheduled it will transfer the correct number of bytes. If however, the occam harness is being used to control a number of processes which have been written in alien languages, then there is no way to check that the transfer is consistent. We believe that the microcode of the transputer for the IN and OUT instructions could be improved. It is almost as if the microcode was different at some stage and that location −2 had been used to store something. We suggest that this location could be used to store the count when a process is descheduled and that the microcode of the second process checks that the counts are consistent: if they are not it should set the error flag.

4.3.2 Pipeline Example

This example shows how GUY can be used to input and output from channels which have a protocol attached to them. It also illustrates a reported bug in the product release of the GUY/occam compiler.

The compiler should leave three free locations below each process which uses input or output, for use if the process is descheduled. However, the compiler only leaves two free locations if a GUY procedure is followed by an occam procedure. In all other cases it creates the workspaces correctly. Thus, an extra unused variable *Dummy* is required in the pipeline example or the system will crash. This extra unused variable should be placed between the call to the GUY and the occam processes.

Within a PAR construct the procedures can appear in any order, and it would have been possible to place them in such an order that the extra unused variable is not required; but equally there are many combinations where extra variables are required and this example has been constructed to bring the bug to your attention and to save you many hours of exasperation.

```
#USE userio
VAL MaxBufferSize IS 512:
PROC Buffer(CHAN OF INT::[]BYTE In, Out)
  INT  Size:
  [MaxBufferSize]BYTE Message:
  GUY
    LDLP  Size      -- load pointer to Size
    LDLP  In        -- load pointer to In
    LDC   4         -- input Size
    IN
    LDLP  Message   -- load pointer to Message
    LDLP  In        -- load pointer to In
    LDL   Size      -- input message
    IN
    LDLP  Size      -- load pointer to Size
    LDLP  Out       -- load pointer to Out
    LDC   4         -- output Size
    OUT
    LDLP  Message   -- load pointer to Message
    LDLP  Out       -- load pointer to Out
    LDL   Size      -- output message
    OUT
  :


[5]CHAN OF INT::[]BYTE Pipe:
VAL OutputString  IS "Well done":
[MaxBufferSize]BYTE Message:
INT Size, Any:
SEQ
  PAR
    Pipe[0] ! (SIZE OutputString):: OutputString
    Buffer(Pipe[0],Pipe[1])
    Buffer(Pipe[1],Pipe[2])
    INT Dummy:
    Pipe[4] ? Size::Message
    Buffer(Pipe[2],Pipe[3])
    Buffer(Pipe[3],Pipe[4])
  write.full.string (screen, "*c*nMessage received :")
  write.len.string(screen, Size, Message)
  keyboard ! Any
```

Figure 4.9. Pipeline example.

In the example shown in figure 4.9, input and output have been combined into one process, but it would be trivial to produce two processes, one to input a message and one to output a message.

Procedures like this are used in parallel C, Pascal and FORTRAN to enable these sequential languages to use channels as in occam. In these systems, the communication procedures are contained in linkable libraries which are called from within tasks (mini programs) and a run-time support system is provided to set up and load the communicating tasks. In the *Buffer* procedure the protocol INT::[]BYTE is executed explicitly. That is, an integer is read in indicating the number of bytes to follow, then that number of bytes is transferred.

Note that pointers to the channel words *In* and *Out* are placed in the workspace when the process *Buffer* is instantiated. However, GUY insists that LDLP In is used, but converts this to LDL In.

4.3.3 Channel Switching

This example is designed to show you how to switch channels from one process to another. Although this is against the principles of occam it is sometimes quite a useful thing to do. This approach could be used in the TDS filer. Initially when files are opened or created this is done by a single process which ALTs on the filer channels. If the opening operations are successful then these channels are passed over to another process which runs in parallel with the original. When the I/O is complete, control is passed back to the original ALT process. This enables the filer to handle a number of files simultaneously. To get a flavour for how this may be done consider figure 4.10.

This program sets up three processes: *Source*, *P1* and *P2*. *Source* sends a string out on the channel *FromSource*. Officially, this data can only be read in by *P1*. However, in this program, the address of the channel word for *FromSource* is passed from *P1* to *P2*, enabling both processes to access the channel. This situation is shown in figure 4.11.

Occam does not enable the user to find out the exact location of the channel word used in communication. This has to be done in assembly language by the procedure *ChannelToChannelId*. Once a pointer to the channel word has been obtained using *ChannelToChannelId* in the *P1* process, it can be sent to process *P2* over the channel *P1ToP2*, enabling it to use the channel *FromSource*. Although this breaks the occam principle that no more than two processes should share a single channel, the synchronisation of the channel is maintained in this exam-

```
PROC Source(CHAN OF BYTE Out)
  VAL str IS "first?second?":
  SEQ i = 0 FOR SIZE str
    Out ! str[i]
:


PROC P1(CHAN OF BYTE FromSource, CHAN OF INT ToP2,FromP2)
  PROC ChannelToChannelId(CHAN OF BYTE Comms,
                          INT ChannelId)
    GUY
      LDLP Comms        -- get pointer to channel
      STL  ChannelId    -- return pointer in ChannelId
  :


  INT ChannelId, Any:
  BYTE Char:
  SEQ
    ChannelToChannelId(FromSource, ChannelId)
    FromSource ? Char
    WHILE Char <> '?'
      SEQ
        ... do something with inputted chars
        FromSource ? Char
    ToP2 ! ChannelId
    FromP2 ? Any
  :


PROC P2(CHAN OF INT FromP1, CHAN OF INT ToP1)
  #USE userio
  INT ChannelId, Any:
  BYTE Char:
  PROC  RxByte(VAL INT ChanId, BYTE Ptr)
    GUY
      LDLP Ptr    -- load pointer to location to
                  -- store byte
      LDL  ChanId -- load pointer to shared channel
      LDC  1      -- transfer one byte
      IN
  :
```

Figure 4.10. An example of how to swap channels between processes.

```
SEQ
  FromP1 ? ChannelId
  Char := 0
  WHILE Char <> '?'
    SEQ
      RxByte(ChannelId, Char)
      write.char(screen,' ')
      write.char(screen, Char)
  keyboard ! Any
  ToP1 ! Any
:
CHAN OF BYTE FromSource:
CHAN OF INT P1ToP2, P2ToP1:
PAR
  Source(FromSource)
  P1(FromSource, P1ToP2, P2ToP1)
  P2(P1ToP2, P2ToP1)
```

Figure 4.10. (cont).

ple by the use of channels *P1ToP2* and *P2ToP1*. The difference is that the synchronisation must be done by the programmer and not by the system.

When the *P2* process receives the pointer to the channel word, it cannot use it in occam to access the channel; this has to be done in assembly language using the procedure *RxByte*.

When the program is run, the string "first" is sent to the process *P1* and the string "second" is sent to process *P2*. The "?" is used to synchronise the use of the channel. This example shows how two very simple assembly language programs can be used to accomplish things that cannot be done in occam, but which may be useful in writing an operating system—even one as simple as TDS.

4.4 Description and Examples Using the ALT Instructions

The first part of this section will show how the ALT instructions work. These instructions were investigated using a program similar to that discussed in section 4.3.1. The results of the investigation are given in the next section, and an example of how to encode a simple replicated

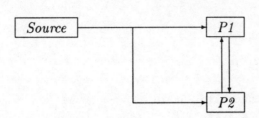

Figure 4.11. The *FromSource* channel is shared between processes *P1* and *P2*.

ALT is given in section 4.4.2. To make this example a little different, we have chosen not to implement the replicated ALT exactly, but to devise a procedure which just returns to the caller which channel is ready for input. Procedures similar to this are used in parallel C, Pascal and FORTRAN.

4.4.1 Implementation of the ALT Instructions

The code used to implement an occam ALT always takes the same format; the ALT is initialised by an ALT or TALT instruction, each guard is then enabled by one of the enable instructions ENBC, ENBS, ENBT. Then the ALTWT or TALTWT instruction is called, which deschedules the current process if none of the guards has fired. A guard is said to have fired when all the conditions are satisfied: either channel input has been available, or a specified time has been reached. The process is rescheduled when one of the channels is ready or a time has been reached, then one of the disable instructions DISC,DISS or DIST is used to disable each guard. Finally, the ALTEND instruction is used to transfer control to the process whose guard has fired. To keep it simple, the sequence of events using ALT, ENBC, ALTWT, DISC and ALTEND is discussed below.

The only action of the ALT instruction is to initialise location −3 of the workspace to *MinInt*+1.

The ENBC instruction looks at the contents of register A, which should contain the boolean part of the guard. If this is *false*, then control passes to the next instruction. If however, register A contains *true*, ENBC then checks if there is any input ready on the channel pointed to by the contents of register B. If the channel is ready to input, then location −3 of the workspace is set to *MinInt*+3 and control passes onto the next instruction. If the channel is not ready to input, then the channel word will be in one of two states: it will either contain *MinInt* or it will point to the current process. If it contains *MinInt* then its contents are altered so that it now points to the workspace of the current ALT process. However, if the channel word already points to the workspace of the current process then no action is required. This last situation will only occur if the same channel occurs in a number of guards.

It may be clearer to reconsider these actions in another way. The ENBC instruction may alter the contents of location −3 of its own workspace and/or it may change the contents of the channel word pointed to by the B register. Each of these changes can only take place if the A register contains *true*, that is if the boolean part of the guard is true. Location −3 is changed from *MinInt*+1 to *MinInt*+3, if the channel word indicates that another process is ready to output on that channel. In this case the channel word is left unchanged, whereas the channel word is changed from *MinInt* to point to the ALT process if the other process is not ready to communicate.

The ALTWT instruction sets location 0 of the workspace to −1. The process is descheduled if location −3 of the workspace contains *MinInt*+1, otherwise it continues on to the next instruction. If the process is descheduled then location −3 is changed to *MinInt*+2 and it will only be rescheduled when another process is ready to output on an enabled channel.

If another process tries to output to the ALT on a channel which has not been enabled, it will find the channel word set to *MinInt* and it will thus deschedule itself after storing its process descriptor in the channel word. If the outputting process finds that the channel word contains a workspace pointer, then the situation is much more complex. When the OUT instruction is executed it must look at location −3 of the workspace of the other process to see whether it is dealing with an ALT process or a straightforward inputting process. If the OUT is communicating with an ALT then location −3 of the ALTs workspace will contain *MinInt*+1, *MinInt*+2 or *MinInt*+3.

If location −3 of the workspace of the ALT process contains *MinInt*+1 then this indicates that the ALT process has not yet reached the ALTWT instruction. In this case location −3 is changed to *MinInt*+3. This can happen if the ALT process has been interrupted by a high priority process and the OUT is either part the interrupting process or it is part of another high priority process which can now run. It can also happen if the ALT process was descheduled by a LEND instruction in a replicated

ALT. If the OUT process was called from a high priority process, the the ALT process will be returned to when no other high priority processes can run. If however, the ALT process was descheduled by a LEND instruction it will be on the active queue and it will be rescheduled when its turn comes.

If location −3 of the workspace of the ALT process contains *MinInt*+2 then the ALT process has executed an ALTWT and the ALT process must be rescheduled by the OUT process, and again location −3 of the ALT workspace must be changed to *MinInt*+3. If however, location −3 of the workspace of the ALT process already contains *MinInt*+3 then the OUT process stores its process descriptor in the channel word. In all cases the OUT process deschedules itself, placing its instruction pointer at location −1, a pointer to the message buffer at location −3 of its own workspace, and a pointer to its workspace is placed in the channel word.

The DISC instruction looks at the contents of the B register which should indicate the state of the boolean part of the guard. If the B register contains *false*, control passes onto the next instruction.

Otherwise it looks at the channel word pointed to by the C register. If the channel word contains *MinInt*, then control passes onto the next instruction, else if it contains the process descriptor of the current process, it stores *MinInt* in the channel word; otherwise the channel word must contain a process descriptor for another process. In this case, if location 0 of the local workspace contains the value −1, then the contents of the A register are placed into location 0 of the workspace. The A register contains the offset to the code of the guarded process from the first instruction past the ALTEND instruction. If control has reached past the ALTWT then one of the DISCs must fire unless another process has illegally altered one of the boolean guards. This is impossible in occam but it could be done in assembly language.

The ALTEND instruction should only be reached if one of the DISCs has fired. In any case it adds the contents of location 0 of the workspace to the program counter and passes control to that point.

4.4.2   Example of an ALT-like Procedure

The example in figure 4.12 shows how a GUY procedure can be written to implement an ALT-like procedure. An array of channels is passed to this procedure and it returns the identity of the input channel that is ready, but no input is performed. Any input is done after the procedure call. 3L use this approach in their implementations of parallel C, FOR-

```
#USE userio
[10]CHAN OF INT Comms:
PROC Alt([]CHAN OF INT Input, INT ChannelId)
  INT Test, LoopTop, LoopIndex, Temp:
  GUY
    ALT                 -- initialize ALT
    LDC  0              -- initialize Test
    STL  Test
    LDC  0              -- initialize replication
    STL  LoopIndex      -- variable to 0
    LDL  (SIZE Input)-- set number of times to replicate
    STL  LoopTop        -- to actual size of Input array
    LDL  LoopTop        -- check for zero sized array
    MINT
    CSUB0
    CJ   .L2            -- if zero jump to L2
    :L1
    LDL  LoopIndex      -- check array indexing
    LDL  (SIZE Input)
    CSUB0               -- if out of range set error flag
    LDLP Input          -- load channel word from Input array
    WSUB
    LDC  1              -- boolean guard always TRUE
    ENBC                -- leaves FALSE in A reg if guard
    LDL  Test           -- does not fire, TRUE otherwise
    OR                  -- OR with current value of Test
    STL  Test
    LDLP LoopIndex      -- point to loop index
    LDC  18             -- number of bytes between L2 and L1
    LEND                -- loop if index below top
    :L2
    LDL  Test           -- if Test contains 0 error in ALT
    LDC  1              -- no guards have fired
    CCNT1               -- if so set error flag
    ALTWT
    LDC  0              -- re-initialize loop variable to 0
    STL  LoopIndex
    LDL  (SIZE Input)-- initialize LoopTop
    STL  LoopTop        -- to actual size of Input array
    LDL  LoopTop        -- check if zero sized array
```

Figure 4.12. Example implementation of ALT-like procedure.

```
        MINT
        CSUB0
        CJ   .L5            -- if so skip
        :L3
        LDL  LoopIndex      -- check array indexing
        LDL  (SIZE Input)
        CSUB0               -- if out of range set error flag
        LDLP Input          -- load channel word from Input array
        WSUB
        LDC 1               -- boolean guard always TRUE
        LDC 0               -- offset from ALTEND
        DISC                -- disable channel
        CJ  .L4
        LDL  LoopIndex      -- return current loop index
        STL  ChannelId      -- in ChannelId
        :L4
        LDLP LoopIndex      -- point to loop index
        LDC  19             -- number of bytes between L5-L3
        LEND                -- loop if index below top
        :L5
        ALTEND


    :
INT ChannelId, Any:
SEQ
  PAR
    INT Num:
    SEQ
      Alt (Comms, ChannelId)
      Comms[ChannelId] ? Num
    INT Dummy:
    INT Id, Ch:
    SEQ
      keyboard ? Ch
      Id := (INT  Ch) - (INT '0')
      IF
        (Id >= 0) AND (Id <=  9)
          Comms[Id] ! Id
  write.full.string (screen, "Channel used was ")
  write.int (screen, ChannelId, 0)
  keyboard ? Any
```

Figure 4.12. (cont).

TRAN and Pascal. This enables their languages to communicate with other processes which wish to output bytes, words or messages. The programmer is expected to input the correct structure.

Using the explanations of the ALT instructions given in the last section it should be possible to follow the given example without much further discussion. The given code was created by first writing the following piece of occam code

```
ALT i = O FOR Size (Input)
  Input[i] ? Num
    ChannelId := i
```

and then inspecting the code produced by the disassembler in the debugger. The code given here is similar to that obtained from the disassembler. It shows the extra checks planted by the compiler. Some of these checks could be removed for efficiency by an experienced GUY writer.

The variable *Temp* in the Alt procedure is necessary, as the DISC instruction uses location 0 of the workspace to store the offset from the ALTEND of a fired guarded process. In this case the offset is always zero as inputting takes place later. The identity of the ready channel can be returned immediately in *ChannelId* if the guard has fired.

This example also shows how to set up a replicated process. This requires the use of two variables in the workspace, and the LEND instruction. One variable is used to store the current iteration count and the other stores the number of iterations left. LEND expects the offset to the start of the loop to be loaded into the A register, but GUY offers no simple means of loading this value; the programmer has to count back the number of bytes required, taking into account any necessary positive or negative prefix instructions. This is tedious and it is very easy to make mistakes. GUY should be enhanced to perform those arithmetic functions which could be done at compile time.

Note the addition of the unused variable *Dummy* to get over the bug discussed in section 4.3.2. If the order of the procedures in the PAR construct are reversed then the use of the *Dummy* variable would not be necessary. It has been added to remind you that a bug exists in the product release of the compiler if a GUY process which performs input or output is followed by an occam process.

As an exercise you may like to code up an *Alt_no_wait* procedure which returns −1 if no guards have fired otherwise it returns the array identifier of the channel which has fired.

```
#USE userio
VAL INT MaxStackSize IS 2000:
VAL INT StackFrameSize IS 4:
INT Input, Result, StackSpaceLeft, Ch, Any:
PROC Fact( VAL INT Input, INT Result,
           VAL INT StackSpaceLeft)
  [MaxStackSize]INT Stack:

  GUY
    -- set up initial stack frame using passed variables
    AJW  MaxStackSize
    :START        -- start of recursive call
    AJW  -1       -- make space for temporary variable
    LDL  4        -- load StackSpaceLeft
    LDC (StackFrameSize+1) -- load size of stack space
    SUB           -- get current space left
    STL  0        -- save new stack space left in Temp
    LDL  0        -- push StackSpaceLeft onto register stack
    CJ   .ERROR -- if zero no stack space left
    LDL  2        -- push value of Input onto stack
    CJ   .LAST  -- if zero no more recursion required
    -- set up new stack frame
    LDL  0        -- push StackSpaceLeft
    LDL  3        -- push Result
    LDL  2        -- push Input
    ADC  -1       -- Input := Input - 1
    CALL .START -- perform recursive call
    -- returns to this point on return from recursive call
    LDL  2        -- push Input
    LDL  3        -- push current value of Result
    LDNL 0
    MUL           -- multiply them together
 ** LDL  3        -- place this in Result
 ** STNL 0
    J    .PASS  -- return from this recursive call
    :ERROR        --
    SETERR        -- error flag set if no stack space left
    :LAST         -- no more recursion required
    LDC  1        -- push 1
 ** LDL  3        -- push pointer to Result
 ** STNL 0        -- return 1 in Result
    :PASS
```

Figure 4.13. Recursive factorial example.

```
        AJW   1          -- recover space used by Temp
        RET
    :
  SEQ
    Ch := 0
    StackSpaceLeft := MaxStackSize
    write.full.string (screen, "Factorial ")
    read.echo.int (keyboard, screen, Input, Ch)
    Fact (Input, Result, StackSpaceLeft)
    write.full.string(screen, " is ")
    write.int (screen, Result, 0)
    keyboard ? Any
```

Figure 4.13. (cont).

4.5   An Example of Recursion Within a GUY Construct

The example in figure 4.13 shows that with the use of GUY, recursive procedures can be performed within occam. The declaration of the local array *Stack* provides stack space for the recursive procedure. The amount of stack space left is checked on each iteration and the error flag is set if a stack space overflow is about to occur. This program must be compiled with the *separate.vector.space* option within the compiler set to *false*, as the program assumes that the space reserved by the declaration of *Stack* is part of the workspace and not contained in a separate vector space.

In this case the declaration of the array *Stack* causes the compiler to adjust the workspace by the size of the array, thus a positive adjust workspace has to be used to set up the initial stack frame for the recursive procedure. Unfortunately the variables are no longer in the positions expected by GUY, but it is fairly easy for the programmer to map out the workspace. An example of the workspace after the first recursive call of *fact*(3,*Result*), is shown in figure 4.14. When GUY is being used with numbers to identify the workspace locations rather than variable names, the programmer has to specify the exact transputer code. For example, instead of using STL Result, the instructions LDL 3, STNL 0 have to be used. The creation of code in this mode is closer to the real instruction set. However, the compiler will still plant any required positive or negative prefixes.

offset	value	description
4	2000	*StackSpaceLeft*
3	—	Pointer to *Result*
2	3	*Input*
1	—	Return Address
0	1995	*Temp*
4	1995	*StackSpaceLeft*
3	—	Pointer to *Result*
2	2	*Input*
1	—	Return Address
0	1990	*Temp*

Figure 4.14. The stack after the first internal call of *Fact*.

Most of the code is fairly self explanatory and can easily be understood by checking in the reference section of this book. In particular, it is worthwhile re-reading the information written on CALL. Note that the *Result* parameter is a pointer and that this is copied in each recursive call, thus the value in the location *Result* is altered after each recursive call.

In this example we have repeated the two starred instructions LDL 3 and STNL 0. These instructions have not been placed just once after the PASS label, because the process may be time-sliced out during a J or LEND instruction, causing the values of the A, B and C registers to be undefined.

4.6   Idle Time Example

The example shown in figure 4.15 is possibly the most useful one given in this chapter, in that it enables you to estimate the idle time for a particular transputer; that is, the time spent by the processor waiting for something to do. This is extremely useful if you are trying to utilise the processors to their maximum potential. Again this has to be done in assembly language as occam does not allow you to access the scheduling registers. The view taken in occam is that it is the responsibility of the system to control the scheduling of the processes and not the programmer, and for efficiency this has to be done in hardware rather than in software. Once scheduling is done in hardware, all processes have to be scheduled, including system processes, by the hardware scheduler.

```
#USE userio
PROC IdleTime(INT IdleCount, ExtraCount, Semaphore)
  INT L.IdleCount, L.ExtraCount:
  INT BackLowPtr, FrontLowPtr:
  GUY
    LDC 0                 -- initialize counters
    STL L.IdleCount
    LDC 0
    STL L.ExtraCount

    :REPEAT
    LDL Semaphore         -- read semaphore
    CJ  .END              -- if zero terminate
    LDLP FrontLowPtr      -- read low priority queue registers
    SAVEL
    LDL  FrontLowPtr      -- and compare front one with MinInt
    MINT
    DIFF
    CJ  .INCIC            -- if queue empty inc idle count
    LDL L.ExtraCount      -- otherwise inc extra count
    ADC 1
    STL L.ExtraCount
    J .PASS

    :INCIC
    LDL L.IdleCount       -- inc idle count
    ADC 1
    STL L.IdleCount

    :PASS                 -- add to end of low priority
    LDC 2                 -- active queue
    LDLP 0
    STARTP
    STOPP                 -- deschedule this process
    J  .REPEAT

    :END
    LDL L.IdleCount       -- return counts and finish
    STL IdleCount
    LDL L.ExtraCount
    STL ExtraCount
  :
```

Figure 4.15. Recursive factorial example.

```
--*** processor/memory speed dependent
VAL IdleTimeConstant IS 36326:
VAL ExtraTimeConstant IS 418:
--***

INT IdleCount, ExtraCount, Semaphore:
INT TotalTime, IdleTime, ExtraTime:
TIMER Clock:
INT TimeNow, TimeBefore, Time, Any, Size:

SEQ
  Semaphore := 1
  IdleCount := 0
  ExtraCount := 0
  keyboard ? Size
  Size := Size - (INT '0')
  Clock ? TimeBefore
  PAR
    SEQ
      Clock ? AFTER TimeBefore PLUS (Size * 15625)
      SEQ i = 0 FOR (Size * 1000000)
        SKIP
      Semaphore := 0
    IdleTime(IdleCount, ExtraCount, Semaphore)
  Clock ? TimeNow
  write.full.string (screen,"Total run time (ms):")
  TotalTime := ((TimeNow - TimeBefore)*64)/1000
  write.int(screen,TotalTime,0 )
  write.full.string (screen, "*c*nIdle count:")
  write.int(screen,IdleCount,0)
  write.full.string (screen,"*c*nIdle time:")
  IdleTime := (IdleCount * 1000) / IdleTimeConstant
  write.int(screen, IdleTime, 0)
  write.full.string (screen,"*c*nExtra processing count:")
  write.int(screen,ExtraCount,0)
  write.full.string (screen,"*c*nExtra processing time:")
  ExtraTime := ExtraCount/ExtraTimeConstant
  write.int(screen,ExtraTime,0)
  write.full.string (screen,"*c*nReal processing time:")
  write.int(screen,TotalTime-ExtraTime,0)
```

Figure 4.15. (cont).

In this example program, an extra process is introduced which can examine the process queue. The main objective of this process is to see why it is being run. There are two possibilities, firstly the process may be running because there are no other processes which are active. This is indicated by the process queue being empty. The other possibility is that this process is running when other processes could have been run. This is indicated by the active process queue being non-empty. In this case, another real process could be running and time is being wasted by running this process. Thus the process has to record two counts, one indicating the number of times it has been run when the process queue was empty and another indicating the number of times it has been run when the process queue was non-empty.

It is possible with a bit of experimentation to turn these counts into times. The exact translation will depend upon things such as processor speed, memory speed, and whether internal or external memory is being used.

The sample user process contains two parts: a timer wait simulating dead time and a SKIP loop simulating active processing. Each part can be timed without the *IdleTime* process running; then the *IdleTime* process can be introduced and the program retimed. The extra time is the time wasted by running the *IdleTime* process when the active SKIP process could have been running. This time can be associated with *ExtraCount*. *IdleCount* is equivalent to the time taken by the timer wait process. These counts can now be used in the timing section and the user process replaced by a more realistic process.

This program breaks the normal occam rules in that it shares the variable *Semaphore* and it accesses the process queues. This is possible even with the occam checker turned on as the checker ignores any GUY code. This enables the GUY programmer to write code which does not adhere to the normal rules. The use of the shared variable is necessary to make the execution of the *IdleTime* process as simple and transparent as possible. *Semaphore* is set to the value one at the start of the program and it is set to zero when all the user's processes have terminated. The *IdleTime* process checks the value of *Semaphore* every time it is run; if it has been changed to zero it terminates, returning the two counts *IdleCount* and *ExtraCount*.

If the value of *Semaphore* is still one, it checks the low priority process queue to see if it is empty. If so it increments *IdleCount*, otherwise it increments *ExtraCount*. It then adds itself to the end of the process queue and deschedules itself. If another process has become ready it will become the running process, otherwise the *Idle Time* process will be rescheduled. To add itself to the rear of the active process queue, the **STARTP** instruction is used. This expects the workspace pointer to be in the A register and an offset to the process execution address in the B register. In this case the offset is to the instruction after the **STOPP** instruction. The **STARTP** instruction is normally used to transfer control to one of a number of parallel processes, but in this case it is used to restart itself when it becomes the running process. The **STOPP** process terminates the current process. This is normally used when an error or exception condition is reached, but it is used in this case to force a process change.

In this example, it assumes that all the processes are low priority. If there were also high priority processes it would make no difference. The high priority processes would be real processes and if they pre-empted this process it would be because they have real work to do, but if they were waiting, for example, for a channel communication then the *Idle Time* process could be run, indicating that no other high or low priority processes were active.

The current program uses integers to hold the counts; however, the *Idle Time* process can be called a large number of times and it is possible for these counts to overflow. The program could be rewritten with the counts held in **INT64**s. This would make it more useful, but it also makes the program longer and adds complications which mask the original concepts; nevertheless it is fairly easy to implement. Remember that **INT64**s are passed to procedures by reference and that they are stored in memory with the least significant 32 bits lower in memory than the most significant 32 bits.

4.7   Simple Loader

The loader program given in figure 4.16 shows how a transputer may initialise a second transputer over an external link, transfer a separately compiled (SC) process to it, and pass control to that SC process. One possible use for this program is to load the kernel of an operating system which will then control the use of the local transputer and pass messages or programs through it to other transputers.

To simplify the discussion we use the loader to load the code of a very simple SC program onto the second transputer. This just echoes characters back to the program running on the first transputer. The program

```
#USE userio
CHAN  OF ANY Out, In:
PLACE Out AT 2:
PLACE In AT 6:
VAL BootStrap IS
-- INT Index, Count, BootChan, EntryPt, LoadPt, PktSize
[#D2 (BYTE),              -- STL BootChan --save
 #D2 (BYTE),              -- STL BootChan --replace
 #D2 (BYTE),              -- STL BootChan --replace by
                                          --pointer to
                                          --boot channel
 #24 (BYTE),#F2 (BYTE), -- MINT            --initialize
                                          --low priority
 #21 (BYTE),#FC (BYTE), -- STLF           --queue
 #24 (BYTE),#F2 (BYTE), -- MINT
 #21 (BYTE),#F7 (BYTE), -- STLB
 #24 (BYTE),#F2 (BYTE), -- MINT           --initialize high
 #21 (BYTE),#F8 (BYTE), -- STHF           --priority queue
 #24 (BYTE),#F2 (BYTE), -- MINT
 #25 (BYTE),#F0 (BYTE), -- STHB
 #25 (BYTE),#F8 (BYTE), -- SETHALTERR     --set halt on
                                          --error flag
 #22 (BYTE),#F9 (BYTE), -- TESTERR        --clear error flag
 #40 (BYTE),            -- LDC 0          --SEQ i = 0 FOR 11
 #D0 (BYTE),            -- STL Index
 #4B (BYTE),            -- LDC 11
 #D1 (BYTE),            -- STL Count      --initialize 11
                                          --locations
 #24 (BYTE),#F2 (BYTE), -- MINT           --to MinInt
 #70 (BYTE),            -- LDL Index      --starting at
                                          --MinInt;
 #24 (BYTE),#F2 (BYTE), -- MINT           --these include
 #FA (BYTE),            -- WSUB           --link, event and
 #E0 (BYTE),            -- STNL 0         --timer registers
 #10 (BYTE),            -- LDLP Index
 #4B (BYTE),            -- LDC 11
 #22 (BYTE),#F1 (BYTE), -- LEND
 #24 (BYTE),#F2 (BYTE), -- MINT           --calculate
 #22 (BYTE),#20 (BYTE),                   --location to start
 #80 (BYTE),            -- ADC 512        --loading code
 #D4 (BYTE),            -- STL LoadPt     --entry point
 #74 (BYTE),            -- LDL LoadPt     --is same as
 #D3 (BYTE),            -- STL EntryPt    --start of code
```

Figure 4.16. Simple loader example.

```
                              -- :LOAD
    #15 (BYTE),               -- LDLP PktSize  --read in size of
    #72 (BYTE),               -- LDL BootChan  --next packet
    #44 (BYTE),               -- LDC 4
    #F7 (BYTE),               -- IN
    #75 (BYTE),               -- LDL PktSize    --reload packet
    #AA (BYTE),               -- CJ .Transfer  --size; if zero
                                               --transfer control
    #74 (BYTE),               -- LDL LoadPt     --at current
                                               --load point
    #72 (BYTE),               -- LDL BootChan  --load packet
    #75 (BYTE),               -- LDL PktSize
    #F7 (BYTE),               -- IN
    #75 (BYTE),               -- LDL PktSize    --increment load
    #74 (BYTE),               -- LDL LoadPt     --pointer by
                                               --packet size
    #F2 (BYTE),               -- BSUB
    #D4 (BYTE),               -- STL LoadPt
    #60 (BYTE),#00 (BYTE),    -- J .LOAD        --get size of
                                               --next packet
                              -- :TRANSFER
    #40 (BYTE),               -- LDC 0          --initialize
    #25 (BYTE),#F4 (BYTE),    -- STTIMER        --timer;
    #73 (BYTE),               -- LDL EntryPt    --load workspace
    #23 (BYTE),#FC (BYTE),    -- GAJW           --pointer for SC
    #33 (BYTE),               -- LDNL EntryPt   --load Entry
                                               --pointer for SC
    #F6 (BYTE)]:              -- GCALL          --transfer to SC


VAL TestProgram IS
    [#60 (BYTE),#BD (BYTE),-- AJW -3
    #11 (BYTE),               -- LDLP 1         --load pointer to Ch
    #24 (BYTE),#F2 (BYTE),    -- MINT           --construct pointer to
    #54 (BYTE),               -- LDNLP 4        --MinInt + 4
    #44 (BYTE),               -- LDC 4          --i.e. input on Link0
    #F7 (BYTE),               -- IN
    #24 (BYTE),#F2 (BYTE),    -- MINT           --output ch
    #71 (BYTE),               -- LDL 1          --on link0
    #FF (BYTE),               -- OUTWORD        --this uses location
                                               --0 of WS
    #60 (BYTE),#04 (BYTE),    -- J -12          --WHILE TRUE
    #B3 (BYTE),               -- AJW 3
    #22 (BYTE),#F0 (BYTE)]:-- RET
```

Figure 4.16. (cont).

```
BYTE BootStrapSize:
INT TestProgramSize:
SEQ
  -- reset second transputer
  BootStrapSize := BYTE(SIZE BootStrap)
  TestProgramSize := (SIZE TestProgram)
  Out ! BootStrapSize :: BootStrap
  Out ! TestProgramSize :: TestProgram
  Out ! 0
  PAR
    INT Ch:
    SEQ
      Ch := 0
      WHILE Ch <> (INT '.')
        SEQ
          keyboard ? Ch
          Out ! Ch
    INT Ch:
    SEQ
      Ch := 0
      WHILE Ch <> (INT '.')
        SEQ
          In ? Ch
          write.char(screen, BYTE Ch)
```

Figure 4.16. (cont).

running on the first transputer reads a character from the keyboard, sends it to the second transputer, waits for it to be echoed and then prints the returned character on the screen. The program terminates when a '.' character is input.

When a transputer receives a hardware reset, (and if its *BootFrom-ROM* pin is set low), it expects to receive a byte from a link. If this byte has a value greater than 1 it assumes that this number is the size of the bootstrap code. It then loads that number of bytes into memory starting at *MemStart* (#80000048 for T414 and #80000070 for the T800), sets the workspace pointer to point to the first word boundary past the end of the bootstrap code and then runs the bootstrap code.

In this program the bootstrap code is included as a BYTE array which is transferred out of link 2 after the second transputer has been reset. The reset code has not been given as it may vary from system to system. In some cases it is possible to manually reset the second transputer. Both

the *Bootstrap* code and the SC code, *TestProgram*, were developed using
GUY and manually copied into this program. It would be possible to
make the program extract the code from any SC and download this to
the second transputer but this would require the use of many of the
features of the TDS which are beyond the scope of this book.

It is assumed that the workspace for this SC will reside in memory
below its program code area. Since control cannot be switched to the
loaded SC until the bootstrap code has finished, the SC must be loaded
above the bootstrap's code and workspace. If the workspace for the SC
is less than the space occupied by the bootstrap then a small amount
of memory will not be used. However, it is usually the case that the
workspace of the SC is larger than the bootstrap's code and workspace,
and will thus reuse all of the space required by the bootstrap. In the
example, the workspace size has been set arbitrarily at 512 for simplicity.
This is larger than required for the SC, and is also larger than the size
of the bootstrap code plus its workspace.

Let us now look at the code in more detail. After the transputer
has been reset and it has downloaded the boot code, the identity of the
channel from which it booted is held in the C register. Thus the three
STLs are required to retrieve its value. The old values of the A and
B registers are required for analysis purposes and not by the bootstrap
code, thus their values are discarded by the first two STLs. The next
requirement is to initialise the front low and high priority queues by
setting their front and back registers to *MinInt*. This indicates that the
queues are empty. Next the error flag is initialised and the transputer
is set to halt if an error occurs. Since the four output link registers, the
four input link registers, the event register, and the low and high priority
timer queue registers are memory mapped into the first 11 locations of
memory, the next action is to set the first eleven locations from *MinInt* to
MinInt+10 to the value *MinInt*, indicating that none of these resources
are in use.

This program contains another example of how to implement a FOR
loop. Two adjacent locations are required in memory, in this case these
are *Index* and *Count*. The *Index* location is used to store the increasing
index number and count the decreasing count identity. When the LEND
instruction is executed, the A register should contain an offset in bytes
to the start of the loop and the B register should point to the first of the
two loop variables. If *Count* contains a 1 when the LEND instruction
is executed, the next instruction to be executed is the one following
the LEND, otherwise the next instruction is found by decrementing the

instruction pointer by the contents of the A register.

Now that most of the registers have been initialised, the next action is to establish the entry point of the SC. It is assumed that this is known beforehand, as it would be if we were loading the kernel of an operating system. In this case it is assumed that the initial load point of the SC is also the entry point, and it is also assumed to be the initial value of the workspace pointer. This will be adjusted negatively by the SC as it is in all occam processes. The code is now read in from the boot link as a series of packet sizes followed by packets. This process is terminated by a zero packet size.

The final action of the bootstrap is to transfer control to the SC. Before transferring control, the timer is initialised by using the STTIMER instruction with zero in the A register. Control is transferred to the SC using the GAJW and GCALL instructions. Normally, an SC would finish with a RET which would attempt to transfer control back to the calling process. However, it is assumed in this case that the SC never finishes, as would be the case with the kernel of an operating system. This is just as well, as the original bootstrap code has probably been destroyed by running the SC and no return address was set up. Note the use of the LDL EntryPt before the GAJW and the LDNL EntryPt after it; this is because the GAJW loads the value in *EntryPt* in the original workspace into the new workspace pointer and saves the old workspace pointer in the A register. This is then used by the LDNL EntryPt to refetch into the A register, the value in *EntryPt* in the old workspace. This in turn is used in the GCALL instruction to set up the new instruction pointer. The priority of the SC is the same as the priority of the bootstrap, which is low priority.

We have described a fairly simple bootstrap which is normally used to load a more complicated bootstrap or part of a distributed operating system which hopefully is written in occam.

4.8 Conclusions

This chapter has shown some of the things it is possible to do in machine code, rather than occam. Clearly, most programming should be carried out using occam or another high-level language, but there are some things, especially system-oriented tasks, which just cannot be done without resorting to machine code.

This chapter has also shown that GUY has a number of nice features but it also has a number of limitations and some peculiarities. Having said this, it was possible with a bit of practice to code all of the above examples. The combination of GUY and occam seems to be a good compromise. We feel that the amount of assembly language written should be kept to a minimum and the limitations of GUY should encourage this.

Chapter 5

Reference Section

This chapter provides a detailed functional description of each T414 transputer instruction. At the top of each page there is the instruction's mnemonic, opcode (in hexadecimal), and full name. This is followed by a precise definition of the instruction, using a symbolic representation of what the instruction does. Then comes a description of each instruction, with finally, an example of its use.

The instructions are arranged in alphabetical order for easy access, but a table of instructions sorted by opcode is provided in appendix A, and a list of instructions sorted into groups of similar function is given in appendix D.

The opcode for each instruction is shown in hexadecimal, and represents the byte or bytes required to actually execute that instruction. For the sixteen single-byte instructions with operands (first column in appendix A), the low nibble of the opcode is represented by the letter 'n', so for the instruction 'Load Constant', the mnemonic is 'LDC n', with opcode '4n'. The operand for these instructions can be extended outside the range 0–15 by using the positive and negative prefix instructions, PFIX n and NFIX n.

The set of instructions which do not have operands are formed using the Operate instruction, which interprets its operand as the opcode of a further set of instructions. In this case, the opcode of the instruction as listed in this reference section is that of the Operate instruction, plus possibly a prefix. So, the opcode for the ADD instruction is listed as 'F5', which is equivalent to OPR 5, and the OR instruction is listed as '24 FB', which is equivalent to PFIX 4; OPR #B.

The definitions of the instructions have been attempted with a minimum of special notation. A full list of symbols used in the formal

symbol	meaning
A	top element of evaluation stack
B	middle element of evaluation stack
C	bottom element of evaluation stack
W	workspace pointer
I	instruction pointer
a, b, c, w, i	initial contents the above registers
n	the operand of the instruction
&	word indexing ($a \& i = a + 2^k i$ for some k)
$\&_{byte}$	byte indexing ($a \&_{byte} i \simeq a + i$)
[ ]	word contents of
[ ]$_{byte}$	byte contents of
$\wedge$	bitwise AND
$\vee$	bitwise OR
$\oplus$	bitwise exclusive-OR
$\ll$	shift left x places
$\gg$	shift right x places
MinInt	minimum integer $= 2^{\text{wordlength}-1}$
$-$	a value that is undefined or unimportant

Table 5.1. Symbols used in the formal definitions.

definitions is given in Table 5.1. (This table is duplicated in appendix B for easy access.) Most of these symbols are self explanatory; the ones that require special mention are concerned with addressing.

A transputer address is considered to consist of two components: a word selector, and a byte offset within that word. The byte offset occupies the bottom few bits of the address; all other bits form the word selector. The number of bits used for the byte offset depends on the number of bytes per word. For the T414 and T800 (both 32-bit machines), two bits are used, representing byte offsets 0–3, whereas the T212 (a 16-bit machine) has a 1-bit byte offset, representing offsets in the range 0–1. Normally, memory is accessed in terms of words: for example, consider the ith word in an array of integers. To calculate the address of this word, it is necessary to add i to the word selector component of the address of the array. Let the address of the array be a. Then for the T414, the word address would evaluate as $a + 4i$, whereas for the T212, it would be $a + 2i$. To represent these word indexing operations in a generic manner, we define the operator & , and would

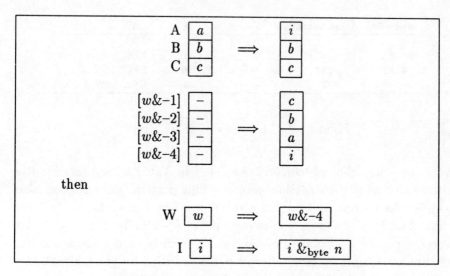

Figure 5.1. A typical formal definition.

thus write the array address as $a\&i$. Think of the $\&$ as standing for 'offset by'.

To access the location pointed to by this address, we use square brackets [ ] to mean 'contents of'. For example, $[a\&i]$ represents the value of the word within the array. The address used by the [ ] operator must have its byte offset bits set to zero, otherwise the effect of the operator is undefined. These two operators together provide for nearly all addressing performed by the transputer.

Sometimes however, the transputer treats memory as a sequence of bytes, for example the sequence of bytes forming the transputer's program. We thus define two further operators: $\&_{\text{byte}}$ and $[\ ]_{\text{byte}}$. The expression $a\&_{\text{byte}}i$ is loosely equivalent to $a + i$. Formally, what it does is add i to the byte offset component of a; any overflow is added to the word selector. For a transputer with a number of bytes-per-word that is a power of two (this includes all INMOS products to date), this process is equivalent to straight addition. However, for a hypothetical 24-bit transputer (3 bytes per word), $1\&_{\text{byte}}2$ evaluates to 4. The expression $[a]_{\text{byte}}$ refers to the byte selected by the byte offset component of a within the word addressed by the word select component of a.

A typical definition of an instruction is shown in figure 5.1; this is in fact the definition of the Call instruction. The first box (always present) shows what happens to the evaluation stack (A,B and C registers). In this particular case, the initial values of the registers are a, b, c. After

Chapter 5

opcode	mnemonic	C	B	A	W	[w]
		c	b	a	F00	–
60 BF	AJW -1	c	b	a	EFC	–
24 F2	MINT	b	a	80000000	EFC	–
D0	STL 0	–	b	a	EFC	80000000

Figure 5.2. The body of an example.

execution, they change to i, b, c. As listed in Table 5.1 earlier, i is the initial value of the instruction pointer. This particular instruction also modifies the four word locations just below where the workspace pointer points to. This is shown in the second block. Finally, the instruction decrements the workspace pointer by four words, and increments the instruction pointer by a number of bytes specified by the instruction's operand n. This is shown in the third and fourth boxes.

The final part of each instruction page contains an example of the use of the instruction. A typical example is shown in figure 5.2. Numbers within the example are always in hexadecimal, except for the mnemonics, where they are explicitly preceeded by a hash (eg #F00).

These examples try to show what happens to the A,B and C registers and any other pertinent registers or memory locations as each instruction is executed. In the example above, the first line indicates that the initial contents of the A,B and C registers are a, b and c, the initial value of the workspace pointer is the address #F00, and the value of the word pointed to by the workspace pointer is unknown or unimportant. After the first instruction AJW -1 has been executed, the workspace pointer has been moved down one word, so it now has the value #EFC. The value at this address is also unimportant. The next instruction, MINT loads the value #80000000 into the A register, displacing its original contents into B, and B into C. Finally, STL 0 stores the value in the A register at the location pointed to by the workspace pointer, popping B into A and C into B, leaving an undefined value in the C register.

Note the difference between W and [w] on the first line. W is the name of a register—the workspace pointer, w represents the current value of this register, and [w] is the value of the word pointed to by this register.

Note finally that although the formal definitions of the instructions are processor word length independent, the examples are based around a T414, so in the example above, MINT was shown loading the 32-bit value #80000000.

ADC n 8n

Add Constant

$$
\begin{array}{c}
\text{A} \\
\text{B} \\
\text{C}
\end{array}
\begin{array}{|c|}
\hline a \\
\hline b \\
\hline c \\
\hline
\end{array}
\quad \Longrightarrow \quad
\begin{array}{|c|}
\hline a+n \\
\hline b \\
\hline c \\
\hline
\end{array}
$$

Error flag set on arithmetic overflow

Adds a constant to the value contained in the A register. Arithmetic overflow is checked for and the error flag is set if it occurs. The range of the constant may be extended with the negative and positive prefix instructions.

Example

Add #42 to the value at the top of the evaluation stack (which is assumed to contain #FC3).

opcode	mnemonic	C	B	A
		c	b	FC3
24 82	ADC #42	c	b	1005

ADD   F5

Signed Addition

$$
\begin{array}{cc}
\text{A} & \boxed{a} \\
\text{B} & \boxed{b} \\
\text{C} & \boxed{c}
\end{array}
\quad \Longrightarrow \quad
\begin{array}{c}
\boxed{a+b} \\
\boxed{c} \\
\boxed{-}
\end{array}
$$

Error flag set on arithmetic overflow

Returns the result of the signed addition of the two signed values in registers A and B in the A register. Arithmetic overflow is checked for and the error flag is set if it occurs.

Example

Add #32 to #AB

opcode	mnemonic	C	B	A
		c	b	a
23 42	LDC #32	b	a	32
2A 4B	LDC #AB	a	32	AB
F5	ADD	–	a	DD

AJW n

Bn

Adjust Workspace

$$
\begin{array}{ll}
A & \boxed{a} \\
B & \boxed{b} \\
C & \boxed{c}
\end{array}
\quad\Longrightarrow\quad
\begin{array}{l}
\boxed{a} \\
\boxed{b} \\
\boxed{c}
\end{array}
$$

$$
W \;\; \boxed{w} \quad\Longrightarrow\quad \boxed{\;w \;\&\; n\;}
$$

Reserves or releases space in the workspace by adding a constant to the workspace pointer. The constant specifies the number of words to reserve or release. The range of the offset may be extended with the positive and negative prefix operations. Arithmetic overflow is not checked for.

Example

Within the body of a procedure call it is necessary to allocate space for local variables, releasing that space at the end of the call. Suppose we have a routine that requires three words of local storage. The code for this would be as follows. We assume that the local workspace is at location #F00.

opcode	mnemonic	C	B	A	W
		c	*b*	*a*	F00
60 BD	AJW -3	*c*	*b*	*a*	EF4
	$\vdots$				
	; *body of procedure here*				
	$\vdots$				
B3	AJW 3	–	–	–	F00
22 F0	RET				

ALT

24 F3

Alt Start

$$
\begin{array}{cc}
A & \boxed{a} \\
B & \boxed{b} \\
C & \boxed{c}
\end{array}
\implies
\begin{array}{c}
\boxed{a} \\
\boxed{b} \\
\boxed{c}
\end{array}
$$

$$
[w\&{-}3] \quad \boxed{-} \implies \boxed{MinInt{+}1}
$$

This instruction is designed for use in the implementation of the occam ALT construct. It starts an ALT sequence of instructions by initialising the third word below the workspace pointer to *MinInt*+1. This location is used by the various Alt Enable instructions for signalling to the Alt Wait instruction that a guard is ready ('fired') and that there is thus no need to deschedule.

Note: if any of the guards wait on a time, then Timer Alt Start should be used instead.

See also instructions ALTWT, ALTEND, TALT, TALTWT, ENBS, DISS, ENBC, DISC, ENBT and DIST.

Example

Since this instruction is really only meaningful when used along with other ALT instructions, a full example is not given; instead, we will show its effect in isolation. For a discussion of how the various ALT instructions interact, see page 43.

opcode	mnemonic	C	B	A	[w&-3]
		c	b	a	-
24 F3	ALT	c	b	a	80000001

ALTEND   24 F5

Alt End

$$
\begin{array}{ll}
A & \boxed{a} \\
B & \boxed{b} \\
C & \boxed{c}
\end{array}
\quad\Longrightarrow\quad
\begin{array}{l}
\boxed{a} \\
\boxed{b} \\
\boxed{c}
\end{array}
$$

$$
I \;\boxed{i} \quad\Longrightarrow\quad \boxed{i \;\&_{\text{byte}} [w]}
$$

(Note: i is the address of the following instruction.)

This instruction is designed for use in the implementation of the oc-cam **ALT** construct. It is used for transferring control to the selected process at the end of an **ALT** instruction sequence. Its action is to add the contents of the memory word at offset 0 in the local workspace to the instruction pointer, that is to say, perform a relative jump. In an **ALT** instruction sequence, location 0 is used by the **Alt Disable** instructions to specify the offset to the selected process relative to the **Alt End** in-struction. This instruction may also be useful for implementing a jump with a computed offset.

Example

Since this instruction is really only meaningful when used along with other **ALT** instructions, a full example is not given; instead, we will show its effect in isolation. For a discussion of how the various **ALT** instructions interact, see page 43. Suppose the code for this example starts at location #1000, and that location 0 in the local workspace contains the value 3.

opcode	mnemonic	C	B	A	[w]	I
		c	b	a	3	1000
24 F5	ALTEND	c	b	a	3	1005
81	ADC 1			*not executed*		
82	ADC 2			*not executed*		
83	ADC 3			*not executed*		
84	ADC 4	c	b	$a+4$	3	1006

ALTWT   24 F4

Alt Wait

$$
\begin{array}{cc}
A & \boxed{a} \\
B & \boxed{b} \\
C & \boxed{c}
\end{array}
\quad \Longrightarrow \quad
\begin{array}{c}
\boxed{-} \\
\boxed{-} \\
\boxed{-}
\end{array}
$$

$$
[w] \; \boxed{-} \quad \Longrightarrow \quad \boxed{-1}
$$

IF $[w\&{-}3] = MinInt{+}3$
THEN the next instruction is executed
ELSE

$$
[w\&{-}3] \; \boxed{MinInt{+}1} \quad \Longrightarrow \quad \boxed{MinInt{+}2}
$$

and the process is descheduled.

Note: this instruction may cause the process to be descheduled.

This instruction is designed for use in the implementation of the occam ALT construct. It initialises the word at offset 0 in the local workspace to -1. This location is subsequently used by the **Alt Disable** instructions (see DISC, DISS and DIST). It then deschedules the process if the contents of the third word below the workspace $[w\&{-}3]$ are set to $MinInt{+}1$ (indicating that no guards have already fired). If however, this word has the value $MinInt{+}3$ (indicating that a guard is ready), execution is continued with the next instruction.

Note: if any of the guards wait on a time, then **Timer Alt Wait** should be used instead.

Example

Since this instruction is really only meaningful when used along with other ALT instructions, a full example is not given; instead, we will show its effect in isolation. For a discussion of how the various ALT instructions interact, see page 43.

opcode	mnemonic	C	B	A	[w&-3]	[w]
		c	*b*	*a*	80000001	−
24 F4	ALTWT	−	−	−	80000002	−1
	process has been descheduled					

AND   24 F6

bitwise AND

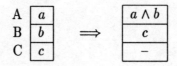

This instruction performs a bitwise AND between the top two operands on the evaluation stack.

Example

Perform an AND between #C2 and #AB

opcode	mnemonic	C	B	A
		c	b	a
2C 42	LDC #C2	b	a	C2
2A 4B	LDC #AB	a	C2	AB
24 F6	AND	–	a	82

BCNT

23 F4

Byte Count

$$
\begin{array}{ll}
A & \boxed{a} \\
B & \boxed{b} \quad \Longrightarrow \\
C & \boxed{c}
\end{array}
\qquad
\boxed{\begin{array}{c}
a\times \ bytes\text{-}per\text{-}word \\
\hline
b \\
\hline
c
\end{array}}
$$

BCNT multiplies the contents of A by the number of bytes in a word (4 for the T414), returning the result in the A register. This instruction may be used for calculating the number of bytes in a given number of words in a manner independent of processor word length.

Example

Calculate the number of bytes in 3 words.

opcode	mnemonic	C	B	A
		c	b	a
43	LDC 3	b	a	3
23 F4	BCNT	b	a	C

BSUB   F2

Byte Subscript

$$
\begin{array}{cc}
A & \boxed{a} \\
B & \boxed{b} \\
C & \boxed{c}
\end{array}
\quad\Longrightarrow\quad
\begin{array}{|c|}
\hline
a \;\&_{\text{byte}}\; b \\
\hline
c \\
\hline
- \\
\hline
\end{array}
$$

This instruction evaluates the address of a byte in a byte array. The base address is in the A register and the byte offset is in the B register. Note that although for the T414 this instruction is merely equivalent to an add instruction, for a transputer with a non-power-of-two number of bytes in a word it would not be (see the section on addressing conventions), so the use of this instruction ensures processor word length independent code (see also WSUB and BCNT).

Example

Find the address of the fifth byte in the byte array starting at address #F02.

opcode	mnemonic	C	B	A
		c	b	a
44	LDC 4	b	a	4
2F 20 42	LDC #F02	a	4	F02
F2	BSUB	$-$	a	F06

CALL n

9n

Call Subroutine

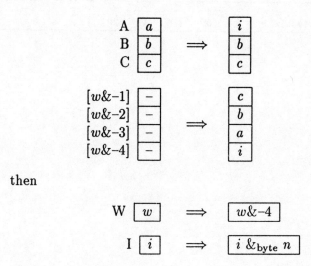

then

$$W \boxed{w} \implies \boxed{w\&-4}$$

$$I \boxed{i} \implies \boxed{i \&_{\text{byte}} n}$$

(Note: i is the address of the following instruction.)

This instruction is used to provide a relative procedure call facility. The workspace pointer is decremented to reserve four words of workspace. The contents of the A, B and C registers are then saved in this area along with the return address. The offset n is then added to the instruction pointer to call the subroutine. (The range of this offset may be extended through the use of positive and negative prefix instructions.)

This instruction is often used when calling a procedure, the last three words of the stack frame required by the procedure being put into the A, B and C registers. Typically in occam, these last three words are the last two parameters to be passed to the procedure (in C and B) and the static link to the lexically enclosing procedure (in A). Further parameters, if required, are placed in the workspace before the Call instruction is executed.

Example

Assume that the workspace pointer contains #B0, that the code starts at location #200, and that a call to a subroutine #14 bytes away is to be performed.

opcode	mnemonic	C	B	A	I	W	[A0]	[A4]	[A8]	[AC]
		c	b	a	200	B0	–	–	–	–
21 94	CALL #14	c	b	202	216	A0	202	a	b	c

CCNT1 24 FD

Check Count From One

$$
\begin{array}{cc}
\text{A} & \boxed{a} \\
\text{B} & \boxed{b} \\
\text{C} & \boxed{c}
\end{array}
\quad \Longrightarrow \quad
\begin{array}{c}
\boxed{b} \\
\boxed{c} \\
\boxed{-}
\end{array}
$$

Error Flag set if $b = 0$ or $b > a$.

Compares the unsigned values in the registers B and A. The error flag is set unless $0 < b <= a$. This instruction is useful for checking array bounds in languages where array indices start from 1.

Example

It is desired to find the address of a word in an array of #20 words stored starting at location 5 in the local workspace. The index is to be found at location 4 in the local workspace. The array starts at index 1 (index 0 being a wasted location) and array bounds are to be checked. We shall assume that the index stored at word location 4 has the value 7, and that the local workspace is at location #F00.

opcode	mnemonic	C	B	A	Error Flag
		c	b	a	–
	; clear error flag				
22 F9	TESTERR	b	a	–	*false*
	; get index				
74	LDL 4	a	–	7	*false*
	; get upper bound of array				
22 40	LDC #20	–	7	20	*false*
	; check that index is in range				
24 FD	CCNT1	–	–	7	*false* (still!)
	; get array base address				
15	LDLP 5	–	7	F14	*false*
	; subscript by word				
FA	WSUB	–	–	F30	*false*

CFLERR

27 F3

Check Floating Point
Infinity or Not-a-Number

$$\begin{array}{c} A \\ B \\ C \end{array} \begin{array}{|c|} \hline a \\ \hline b \\ \hline c \\ \hline \end{array} \implies \begin{array}{|c|} \hline a \\ \hline b \\ \hline c \\ \hline \end{array}$$

Error Flag set if A contains floating point infinity or not-a-number.

Note: this instruction is specific to the T414.

This instruction sets the error flag if the A register contains one of the bit patterns defined as Infinity or Not-a-Number by the IEEE 754 floating point standard. It is intended for use in implementing floating point software packages for the T414.

CJ n An

Conditional Jump

IF $a = 0$ THEN

ELSE

(Note: i is the address of the following instruction.)

If the content of A is *false*, i.e. zero, this instruction performs a jump to a new location by adding the offset n to the instruction pointer. If the jump is taken, the evaluation stack is left unchanged, otherwise the condition on the top of the stack is popped. This asymmetry is useful in calculating boolean expressions. The range of the displacement n may be extended through the use of the positive and negative prefix instructions.

Example

Find whether locations 2 and 3 in the local workspace both contain the value 7. We shall suppose that the content of location 2 is in fact #FF, and that the code fragment starts at location #2000. The first section of the code tests to see if location 2 contains the value 7. (Since it in fact does not, the program skips over the second section of code.) This second section tests location 3 for equality with seven, and if this is the case, performs a relative jump to some other part of the program (CJ n).

opcode	mnemonic	C	B	A	I
		c	*b*	*a*	2000
72	LDL 2	*b*	*a*	FF	2001
C7	EQC 7	*b*	*a*	0	2002
A5	CJ 5	*b*	*a*	0	2008
73	LDL 3	*; this instruction skipped*			
C7	EQC 7	*; this instruction skipped*			
23 F2	NOT	*; this instruction skipped*			
An	CJ n	*; this instruction skipped*			
		; execution continues from this point			

CLRHALTERR 25 F7

Clear Halt-On-Error Flag

$$
\begin{array}{cc}
A & \boxed{a} \\
B & \boxed{b} \\
C & \boxed{c}
\end{array}
\implies
\begin{array}{c}
\boxed{a} \\
\boxed{b} \\
\boxed{c}
\end{array}
$$

Halt-On-Error Flag $\boxed{-}$ $\implies$ $\boxed{false}$

The halt-on-error flag is cleared. This has the effect of putting the transputer into the mode that allows execution to continue if the error flag becomes set.

CSNGL   24 FC

Check Single

$$
\begin{array}{c|c}
A & a \\
B & b \\
C & c \\
\end{array}
\quad\Longrightarrow\quad
\begin{array}{|c|}
a \\
c \\
- \\
\end{array}
$$

IF ($a \geq 0$ and $b \neq 0$) or ($a < 0$ and $b \neq -1$)
THEN *Error Flag* is set

The double word-length signed value in register pair BA (B contains the high order word) is reduced to a single length value in A. If the double length value is not representable in a single word, i.e. if the top (sign) bit of A is not the same as ALL the bits of B, then the error flag is set. The C register is then popped into the B register.

Example

This instruction may be used to convert any multiple word length signed integer to any other smaller multiple. We shall convert a triple length integer stored at offsets 0, 1 and 2 (low to high) in the local workspace into a single length value to be returned at offset 3. The error flag will be set if the triple length value is too large to be represented in one word. We shall suppose that the value of the integer is #00000000,00005743, 749EFA43.

opcode	mnemonic	C	B	A	Error Flag
	; clear error flag	c	b	a	–
22 F9	**TESTERR**	b	a	–	*false*
	; convert highest two words to single word				
72	**LDL 2**	a	–	0	*false*
71	**LDL 1**	–	0	5743	*false*
24 FC	**CSNGL**	–	–	5743	*false* (still)
	; now reduce remaining double length value				
70	**LDL 0**	–	5743	749EFA43	*false*
24 FC	**CSNGL**	–	–	749EFA43	*true*
	; finally store result				
D3	**STL 3**	–	–	–	*true*

CSUB0   21 F3

Check Subscript From
Zero

$$
\begin{array}{c}
A \\ B \\ C
\end{array}
\begin{array}{|c|}
\hline a \\ \hline b \\ \hline c \\ \hline
\end{array}
\implies
\begin{array}{|c|}
\hline b \\ \hline c \\ \hline - \\ \hline
\end{array}
$$

IF ($b \geq_{\text{unsigned}} a$) THEN *Error Flag* is set

Sets the error flag to the result of the unsigned comparison ($b \geq a$). The unsigned comparison used has the same effect as the signed comparison ($b \geq a$ or $b < 0$). The main use for this instruction is in the checking of array bounds. Note that the stack is only popped once—eliminating the bound and leaving the index—to facilitate this.

Example

It is desired to generate the address of a word in an array of #20 words starting at word offset 5 in the local workspace. The index is to be found at word offset 4 in the local workspace. Array bounds are to be checked. The workspace pointer is assumed to contain #F00, and the index is assumed to have the value 7.

opcode	mnemonic	C	B	A	Error Flag
		c	b	a	–
	; clear error flag				
22 F9	TESTERR	b	a	–	*false*
	; get index				
74	LDL 4	a	–	7	*false*
	; get upper bound of array				
22 40	LDC #20	–	7	20	*false*
	; check index is in range				
21 F3	CSUB0	–	–	7	*false* (still)
	; get array base address				
15	LDLP 5	–	7	F14	*false*
	; subscript by word				
FA	WSUB	–	–	F30	*true*

CWORD

Check Word

```
A │ a │        │ b │
B │ b │   ⟹    │ c │
C │ c │        │ - │
```

IF $(b \geq a)$ or $(b < -a)$ THEN *Error Flag* is set

This instruction checks that a single length signed integer in B, will compress to a specified partword. The length of the partword is specified by passing the most negative integer representable by the partword in A (i.e. for a n-bit partword, bit n-1 only should be set). If the integer will not fit into the part word, the error flag is set. The partword length specifier is popped after use.

Example

Add the two signed *five-bit* values that are stored at offsets 0 and 1 in the local workspace and return the result at offset 2. The result is to be checked for overflow beyond the five-bit boundary. It is assumed that the values of the numbers are 8 and −15

Chapter 5

opcode	mnemonic	C	B	A	Error Flag
	; *clear error flag*	c	b	a	–
22 F9	TESTERR	b	a	–	*false*
	; *load first integer*				
70	LDL 0	a	–	8	*false*
	; *extend to word*				
21 40	LDC #10	–	8	10	*false*
23 FA	XWORD	–	–	8	*false*
	; *same for second integer*				
71	LDL 1	–	8	11	*false*
21 40	LDC #10	8	11	10	*false*
23 FA	XWORD	–	8	FFFFFFF1	*false*
	; *add them*				
F5	ADD	–	–	FFFFFFF9	*false*
	; *check for overflow*				
21 40	LDC #10	–	FFFFFFF9	10	*false*
25 F6	CWORD	–	–	FFFFFFF9	*false* (still)
D2	STL 2	–	–	–	*false*

DIFF

F4

Unsigned Subtraction (Difference)

$$
\begin{array}{cc}
A & \boxed{a} \\
B & \boxed{b} \\
C & \boxed{c}
\end{array}
\implies
\begin{array}{|c|}
\hline
b -_{\text{unsigned}} a \\
\hline
c \\
\hline
- \\
\hline
\end{array}
$$

(*Error Flag* is unaffected).

Performs the subtraction $b - a$. Underflow is allowed and the error flag is not affected.

Example

If the value #80000001 is in register B and the value #2 is in register A then the difference will be #7FFFFFFF.

opcode	mnemonic	C	B	A
		c	b	a
28 20 20				
20 20 20				
20 41	LDC #800000001	b	a	800000001
42	LDC 2	a	800000001	2
F4	DIFF	–	a	7FFFFFFF

DISC   22 FF

Disable Channel

Let

a = the offset to the guarded process from the **Alt End** instruction,

b = the result of the boolean part of the guard,

c = the address of the channel word.

$priority$ = the 1-bit value indicating the priority of the current process.

$fired = ((b \neq 0) \text{ AND } ([w] = -1) \text{ AND } ([c] \neq MinInt)$ $\text{AND } ([c] \neq (w \vee priority)))$.

Then the action of the instruction is as follows:

A	a (process offset)	$\Longrightarrow$	$fired$
B	b (boolean)		$-$
C	c (channel)		$-$

IF $fired=true$ THEN

$$[w] \boxed{-1} \quad \Longrightarrow \quad \boxed{a}$$

Additionally,

IF $((b \neq 0) \text{ AND } ([c] = w \vee priority))$ THEN disable channel:

$$[c] \boxed{w \vee priority} \quad \Longrightarrow \quad \boxed{MinInt}$$

This instruction is designed for use in the implementation of the occam **ALT** construct. The instruction takes three parameters: the result of the boolean part of the guard in the B register, the address of the control word of the channel that is to fire the guard in the C register and an offset to the guarded process in the A register. The instruction determines whether or not the guard has fired by inspecting the boolean, the contents of the channel word and the contents of the flag at offset 0 in the local workspace. The guard is deemed to have fired if all of the following conditions are met: the boolean must be *true* (non-zero), the channel control word must indicate a process waiting on that channel (control word not equal to *MinInt*) and the flag in local 0 must indicate that no other guards have already fired (*flag* = −1). If the guard has fired, *true* is returned in A and the offset is stored at local 0, otherwise *false* is returned. It should be noted that no input operation is performed; this must be done by the guarded process.

Example

Since this instruction is really only meaningful when used along with other ALT instructions, a full example is not given; instead, we will show its effect in isolation. For a discussion of how the various ALT instructions interact, see page 43. The following code represents what is required to disable a particular ALT guard. We assume that the channel word lies at location 0 in the local workspace, that the channel is ready to communicate, that no other Disable instruction has yet succeeded ([*w*] = −1), that the guard evaluates to *true*, i.e. 1, and that the offset from where the Alt End lies to where the code for dealing with this guard lies, is 8 bytes. We assume that the local workspace is at location #F00.

opcode	mnemonic	C	B	A	[*w*]
	; load pointer to channel	*c*	*b*	*a*	−1
10	LDLP 0	*b*	*a*	F00	−1
	⋮				
	; evaluate boolean				
	⋮	*a*	F00	1	−1
48	LDC 8	F00	1	8	−1
22 FF	DISC	−	−	1	8

DISS   23 F0

Disable Skip

Let

a = the offset to the guarded process from the **Alt End** instruction,

b = the result of the boolean part of guard,

$fired = ((b \neq 0) \text{ AND } ([w] = -1))$.

Then the action of the instruction is as follows:

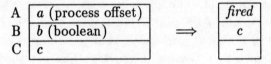

IF *fired=true* THEN

$$[w] \boxed{-1} \implies \boxed{a}$$

This instruction is designed for use in the implementation of the occam **ALT** construct. The instruction takes two parameters: the result of the boolean part of the guard in the B register and an offset to the guarded process in the A register. The instruction determines whether or not the guard has fired by inspecting the boolean value and the contents of the flag at offset 0 in the local workspace. The guard is deemed to have fired if the boolean is *true* (non zero) and if the flag in local 0 indicates that no other guards have already fired (*flag* = -1). If these conditions are met then *true* is returned in A and the offset is stored at local 0, otherwise *false* is returned.

Example

Since this instruction is really only meaningful when used along with other **ALT** instructions, a full example is not given; instead, we will show its effect in isolation. For a discussion of how the various ALT instructions interact, see page 43. The following code represents what is required to disable a particular ALT guard. We assume that no other **Disable** instruction has yet succeeded ($[w] = -1$), that the guard evaluates to *true*, i.e. 1, and that the offset from where the **Alt End** lies to where the code for dealing with this guard is, is 8 bytes.

opcode	mnemonic	C	B	A	[w]
	⋮	c	b	a	−1
	; evaluate boolean				
	⋮	b	a	1	−1
48	LDC 8	a	1	8	−1
22 FF	DISS	−	a	1	8

DIST   22 FE

Disable Timer

Let

a = the offset to the guarded process from the **Alt End** instruction,

b = the result of the boolean part of the guard,

c = the guard's time.

$fired = ((b \neq 0) \text{ AND } ([w] = -1) \text{ AND } (current\ time\ \text{after}\ c)).$

Then the action of the instruction is as follows:

A	a (process offset)			*fired*
B	b (boolean)	$\Longrightarrow$		–
C	c (time)			–

IF *fired=true* THEN

$$[w\&-1]\ \boxed{-1}\ \Longrightarrow\ \boxed{a}$$

Additionally,

IF $((b \neq 0)$ AND ("current time" before c)) THEN
disable timer: remove ALT process from timer queue.

This instruction is designed for use in the implementation of the occam **ALT** construct. The instruction takes three parameters; the result of the boolean part of the guard in the B register, the time at which the guard is to fire in the C register and an offset to the guarded process in the A register. The instruction determines whether or not the guard has fired by inspecting the boolean, the time value and the contents of offset 0 in the local workspace. The guard is deemed to have fired if all of the following conditions are met: the boolean must be *true* (non-zero), the time value must be before the current time, and the flag at location 0 must indicate that no other guards have already fired (*flag* = −1). If the guard has fired, *true* is returned in A, otherwise *false* is returned.

The possibility exists that a timer ALT which is waiting on both a channel and a time might be rescheduled due to input becoming available on the channel. This would mean that a 'phantom' ALT process would still be sitting in the timer queue, ready to be rescheduled when its time comes to pass. To avoid this, the hardware responsible for reactivating processes in the timer queue checks location −3 in their workspace first. If this has the value *MinInt*+3, it implies that the process is an ALT which has already fired on some other event, and so the process is discarded. However, location −3 only holds a valid value up until the end of the ALT construct, so a side-effect of the DIST is that it parses through the timer queue and removes the ALT process from the queue if it can find it.

This instruction may take an arbitrary length of time to execute, since the timer queue may be of arbitrary length. Thus, it has been made interruptable in order to improve interrupt latency for high priority processes.

Example

Since this instruction is really only meaningful when used along with other ALT instructions, a full example is not given; instead, we will show its effect in isolation. For a discussion of how the various ALT instructions interact, see page 43. The following code represents what is required to disable a particular ALT guard. We assume that the current time is past the guard's time, that no other Disable instruction has yet succeeded ($[w] = -1$), that the guard evaluates to *true*, i.e. 1, and that the offset from where the Alt End lies to where the code for dealing with this guard is, is 8 bytes.

opcode	mnemonic	C	B	A	[w]
	; *load guard's time*	*c*	*b*	*a*	−1
4x	LDC *time*	*b*	*a*	*time*	−1
	⋮				
	; *evaluate boolean*				
	⋮	*a*	*time*	1	−1
48	LDC 8	*time*	1	8	−1
22 FE	DIST	−	−	1	8

DIV   22 FC

Divide

$$
\begin{array}{ll}
\text{A} & \boxed{a} \\
\text{B} & \boxed{b} \\
\text{C} & \boxed{c}
\end{array}
\quad\Longrightarrow\quad
\boxed{\begin{array}{c} b/a \\ c \\ - \end{array}}
$$

unless $(a = 0)$ or $(a = -1$ and $b = MinInt)$, in which case

$$
\begin{array}{ll}
\text{A} & \boxed{a} \\
\text{B} & \boxed{b} \\
\text{C} & \boxed{c}
\end{array}
\quad\Longrightarrow\quad
\boxed{\begin{array}{c} \text{undefined} \\ c \\ - \end{array}}
$$

$$
\text{Error Flag} \quad \boxed{-} \quad \Longrightarrow \quad \boxed{true}
$$

Returns the result of an integer divide of the top two values on the evaluation stack. The error flag is set and an undefined result is returned if division by zero is attempted, or if the result would overflow.

Example

Divide #20 by 4.

opcode	mnemonic	C	B	A
		c	b	a
22 40	LDC #20	b	a	20
44	LDC 4	a	20	4
22 FC	DIV	$-$	a	8

ENBC 24 F8

Enable Channel

Let

a = the boolean part of the guard,
b = the address of the channel word,
priority = the 1-bit value indicating the priority of the current process.

A	a (boolean)		a
B	b (channel)	$\Longrightarrow$	c
C	c		—

IF $a = false$ THEN guard not enabled; do nothing;
ELSE

IF $[b] = MinInt$ THEN no process is waiting on the channel, so initiate communication:

$$[b] \boxed{MinInt} \quad \Longrightarrow \quad \boxed{w \vee priority}$$

ELSE IF $[b] = w \vee priority$ THEN another guard of the current process is waiting on the channel; do nothing;

ELSE another process is waiting on the channel, so set a flag to show that the guard is ready:

$$[w\&-3] \boxed{-} \quad \Longrightarrow \quad \boxed{MinInt+3}$$

This instruction is designed for use in the implementation of the occam ALT construct. The instruction takes two parameters: the result of the boolean part of the guard in the A register and the address of the control word of the channel that is to fire the guard in the B register. The instruction determines whether or not the guard has fired by inspecting the boolean and the contents of the channel word. The guard is deemed to have fired if the following conditions are met: the boolean must be *true* (non zero) and the channel control word must indicate a process (other than another guard of the same ALT) waiting on that channel (control word not equal to *MinInt*). If the guard has fired, the flag at location $[w\&-3]$ is set to *MinInt*+3 to signal to the following Alt Wait instruction that a guard has already fired. If no process is waiting on the channel (control word equal to *MinInt*) and the boolean is *true*, the current process descriptor is written into the channel control word. The instruction leaves the result of the boolean part of the guard in the A register to allow the inclusion of code to check that at least one ALT guard has a *true* boolean part.

Example

Since this instruction is really only meaningful when used along with other ALT instructions, a full example is not given; instead, we will show its effect in isolation. For a discussion of how the various ALT instructions interact, see page 43. The following is just a simple example showing typical code produced to enable a channel whose word is at location 2 in the local workspace, and whose boolean part of the guard is *true*. We assume that the local workspace is at location #F00.

opcode	mnemonic	C	B	A
		c	*b*	*a*
12	LDLP 2	*b*	*a*	F08
41	LDC *true*	*a*	F08	1
24 F8	ENBC	–	*a*	1

ENBS   24 F9

Enable Skip

Let

a = the boolean part of the guard.

Then

$$
\begin{array}{c}
\text{A} \\ \text{B} \\ \text{C}
\end{array}
\begin{array}{|l|}
\hline a\ (\text{boolean}) \\ \hline b \\ \hline c \\ \hline
\end{array}
\quad \Longrightarrow \quad
\begin{array}{|l|}
\hline a \\ \hline b \\ \hline c \\ \hline
\end{array}
$$

IF $a = true$ THEN set a flag to show that the guard is ready:

$$
[w\&{-}3]\ \boxed{\ -\ } \quad \Longrightarrow \quad \boxed{\ MinInt{+}3\ }
$$

This instruction is designed for use in the implementation of the occam ALT construct. The instruction takes one parameter: the result of the boolean part of the guard in the A register. The boolean is left in the A register at the completion of the instruction. If the boolean is *true*, the flag word at offset -3 in the local workspace is set to *MinInt*+3, otherwise this location is left unaffected.

Example

Since this instruction is really only meaningful when used along with other ALT instructions, a full example is not given; instead, we will show its effect in isolation. For a discussion of how the various ALT instructions interact, see page 43.

opcode	mnemonic	C	B	A	[$w\&{-}3$]
		c	b	a	–
41	LDC *true*	b	a	1	–
24 F9	ENBS	b	a	1	80000003

ENBT   24 F7

Enable Timer

Let

a = the boolean part of the guard,
b = the time to wait until for this guard.

A	a (boolean)		a
B	b (time)	$\Longrightarrow$	c
C	c		$-$

IF $a = false$ THEN guard not enabled; do nothing;
ELSE

IF $[w\&{-}4] = MinInt{+}2$ THEN no previous time has been
stored, so store the time value and set the flag:

$[w\&{-}4]$	$MinInt{+}2$	$\Longrightarrow$	$MinInt{+}1$
$[w\&{-}5]$	$-$		b

ELSE IF ($[w\&{-}5]$ AFTER b) THEN store new time:

$[w\&{-}5]$	*old time*	$\Longrightarrow$	b

The purpose of this instruction is to find the earliest time that is to
be waited for within a Timer ALT sequence. Location $[w\&{-}5]$ is used
to record this time, and contains a flag indicating whether the time is
valid (i.e. whether at least one time value has been stored there). One
of the effects of the Timer Alt Wait instruction is to initialise $[w\&{-}4]$
to $MinInt{+}2$, which indicates an invalid time. Then, for each timer
guard in the ALT construct, the Enable Timer instruction is executed.
This has the effect of storing the time to be waited until for this guard
at location $[w\&{-}5]$, but only if the boolean expression that forms part
of the guard has evaluated to *true*, and the time is earlier than any
previously recorded. If no previous time has been recorded, then the
time is stored, and location $[w\&{-}4]$ is set to $MinInt{+}1$ to indicate a

valid time.

Example

Since this instruction is really only meaningful when used along with other ALT instructions, a full example is not given; instead, we will show its effect in isolation. For a discussion of how the various ALT instructions interact, see page 43. Consider the following occam Timer ALT sequence:

```
ALT
  FALSE & timer AFTER #100
    proc1
  TRUE  & timer AFTER #123
    proc2
  TRUE  & timer AFTER #122
    proc3
  TRUE  & timer AFTER #124
    proc4
```

The values *true* and *false* would normally be the results of a boolean expression, rather than just being constant as in this example. After executing Enable Timer for each guard, the earliest time recorded should be #122, which will be the time to wait until. The initial code generated for this sequence would be as follows:

opcode	mnemonic	C	B	A	[w&–5]	[w&–4]
		c	*b*	*a*	–	–
set flag showing no time set						
24 FE	TALT	*c*	*b*	*a*	–	80000002
first guard: this has no effect since the boolean is false						
21 20 40	LDC #100	*b*	*a*	100	–	80000002
40	LDC *false*	*a*	100	0	–	80000002
24 F7	ENBT	–	*a*	0	–	80000002
second guard: this stores its time because it is the only one so far						
21 22 43	LDC #123	*a*	0	123	–	80000002
41	LDC *true*	0	123	1	–	80000002
24 F7	ENBT	–	0	1	123	80000001
third guard: this stores its time because it is earlier than the last						
21 22 42	LDC #122	0	1	122	123	80000001
41	LDC *true*	1	122	1	123	80000001
24 F7	ENBT	–	1	1	122	80000001
last guard: this doesn't store its time because it's later						
21 22 44	LDC #124	1	1	124	122	80000001
41	LDC *true*	1	124	1	122	80000001
24 F7	ENBT	–	1	1	122	80000001

ENDP F3

End Process

Let

a = the address of the workspace of the parent process,
$[a\&1]$ = number of child processes still active,
$[a]$ = execution address of parent process upon restart.

A	a (workspace)		$-$
B	b	$\Longrightarrow$	$-$
C	c		$-$

IF $[a\&1] = 1$ THEN there are no more child processes; continue as parent process:

$$[a\&1] \quad \boxed{1} \quad \Longrightarrow \quad \boxed{0}$$

$$I \quad \boxed{i} \quad \Longrightarrow \quad \boxed{[a]}$$

$$W \quad \boxed{w} \quad \Longrightarrow \quad \boxed{a}$$

ELSE

$$[a\&1] \quad \boxed{k} \quad \Longrightarrow \quad \boxed{k-1}$$

The current process is terminated, and another process is scheduled from the active queue.

(Note: i is the address of the following instruction.)

The current process is terminated and control is returned to the parent process if all the child processes have terminated. A pointer to the workspace of the successor process is passed in register A. This pointer should point to two words: at $[a]$ is stored the address at which execution is to continue and at $[a\&1]$ is the count of remaining child processes. These two locations should be initialised by the parent process before the children are started. See also **Start Process**. If the count is not 1, it is decremented and another process is selected from the active queues. If however the count is 1, control is transferred to the location specified and the contents of A are transferred to the workspace pointer register.

Example

The current process is to be terminated and control returned to the parent if all children have terminated. Assume the parent's workspace starts at #F00 and that the current number of children is 3.

opcode	mnemonic	C	B	A	[F00]
		c	*b*	*a*	3
2F 20 40	LDC #F00	*b*	*a*	F00	3
F3	ENDP	–	–	–	2

This process is then terminated, and another waiting process is rescheduled.

EQC n   Cn

Equals Constant

$$
\begin{array}{c}
A \\ B \\ C
\end{array}
\begin{array}{|c|}
\hline a \\ \hline b \\ \hline c \\ \hline
\end{array}
\implies
\begin{array}{|c|}
\hline a = n \\ \hline b \\ \hline c \\ \hline
\end{array}
$$

Returns the boolean result of a test for equality between the value in A and the constant n. If a is the same as the value n then *true*, i.e. 1 is stored in A, else *false*, i.e. 0 is stored. This instruction may also be used to perform the NOT operation. An EQC 0 instruction performed when A contains a boolean will return the logical NOT of A. The range of the constant n may be extended with the positive and negative prefix instructions.

Example

Test the second word on the workspace for equality with 7. The location is assumed to contain #7F0.

opcode	mnemonic	C	B	A
		c	b	a
72	LDL 2	b	a	7F0
C7	EQC 7	b	a	0

FMUL 27 F2

Fractional Multiply

Error Flag set if $a = b = MinInt$.

Discussion: It is possible to have a form of integer arithmetic where each integer represents a number between -1 and 1. This is effectively the same as having the 'decimal' (actually binary) point to the right of the leftmost bit. As an example, the following table shows how various values would be represented in this format as 3-bit signed integers.

value (base 10)	base 2 equivalent	3-bit integer representation
-1.00	-1.00	100
-0.75	-0.11	101
-0.50	-0.10	110
-0.25	-0.01	111
0.00	0.00	000
0.25	0.01	001
0.50	0.10	010
0.75	0.11	011

Note the relationship $i = 2^{n-1} f$, where i is the integer representation, f is the fractional number to be represented, and n is the number of bits in the word. Note also that in general, $-1 \leq f < 1$, the asymmetry in the range of f being caused by the usual problem with twos complement representation.

Problems arise when it is required to multiply two numbers of this form together. In general, multiplying two 32-bit numbers together produces a 64-bit result. However, we are usually only interested in the bottom 32 bits of the result, and would regard any excursion into the

higher word as an overflow. This is the way the normal **Multiply** instruction works. However, for fractional numbers this is not the case.
Consider $0.5 \times 0.5 = 0.25$. This would be evaluated as #40000000 $\times$
#40000000 which would clearly cause an overflow. Thus, the instruction
Fractional Multiply is provided. This evaluates $2^{1-\text{wordlength}} \times a \times b$, which
provides a suitably scaled result. There is, in general, no overflow since
products of fractions are still fractional. There is only one exception:
the special case of $-1 \times -1 = 1$, since 1 is not representable. Thus the
error flag will be set only if both operands are equal to *MinInt*, i.e. the
value which represents -1.

GAJW 23 FC

General Adjust Workspace

$$W \boxed{w} \quad \Longrightarrow \quad \boxed{a}$$

$$
\begin{array}{c}
A \\ B \\ C
\end{array}
\boxed{\begin{array}{c} a \\ b \\ c \end{array}}
\quad \Longrightarrow \quad
\boxed{\begin{array}{c} w \\ b \\ c \end{array}}
$$

This instruction exchanges the contents of the A register with the contents of the workspace pointer. It can be used to implement workspace allocation schemes that do not fit into the normal static allocation allowed by the **Adjust Workspace** instruction and in particular, enables the pointer to be set to a specified absolute location in memory.

The address in the A register should have its byte select bits (i.e the bottom two bits in the case of the T414) set to zero. This will normally already be the case if the address has been obtained by using address-manipulation instructions such as **Load Local Pointer** and **Word Subscript**. The effect of executing **GAJW** without these bits set to zero is undefined.

Example

On boot-up, it is usual to have the workspace pointer pointing to the top end of memory, to enable the 'stack' to work downwards. Suppose that the top of memory is at #800FFFFF.

opcode	mnemonic	C	B	A	W
		c	b	a	w
28 20 20					
2F 2F 2F					
2F 4C	LDC #800FFFFC	b	a	800FFFFC	w
23 FC	GAJW	b	a	w	800FFFFC

GCALL   F6

General Call

$$
\text{I} \;\boxed{i} \quad \Longrightarrow \quad \boxed{a}
$$

$$
\begin{array}{ll}
\text{A} & \boxed{a} \\
\text{B} & \boxed{b} \quad \Longrightarrow \quad \\
\text{C} & \boxed{c}
\end{array}
\qquad
\begin{array}{l}
\boxed{i} \\
\boxed{b} \\
\boxed{c}
\end{array}
$$

(Note: i is the address of the following instruction.)

This instruction exchanges the value in the instruction pointer I, with that in register A. This instruction can be used to transfer control to any address, allowing the user complete freedom for addressing calculations etc. The GCALL instruction can also be used to return from a piece of code. When procedure calls are implemented using this instruction rather than with CALL, it is up to the programmer to construct stack frames, save the return address and so on.

Note that it is the address of the instruction *following* the GCALL that is placed in the A register.

Example

It is desired to call a routine at address #C2. The code fragment is assumed to start at address #A7.

opcode	mnemonic	C	B	A	I
		c	b	a	A7
2C 42	LDC #C2	b	a	C2	A9
F6	GCALL	b	a	AA	C2

GT

F9

Greater Than

If $b > a$ then *true* (1) is returned on the stack, otherwise *false* (0) is returned.

Example

It is to be determined whether the second word in the workspace is greater than –1. We shall assume that the said location contains the value 6.

opcode	mnemonic	C	B	A
		c	b	a
71	LDL 1	b	a	6
60 4F	LDC –1	a	6	FFFFFFFF
F9	GT	–	a	1

IN   F7

Input Message

Let

a = the number of bytes to transfer,
b = a pointer to the channel word,
c = a pointer to an area of memory where the data is
   to be transferred.

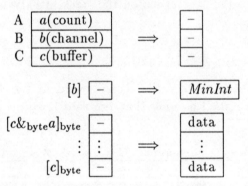

Note: this instruction may cause the process to be descheduled.

This instruction inputs the number of bytes specified by the value in the A register from a channel whose control word is pointed to by the B register, and stores these bytes starting at the address pointed to by the value in register C. All three registers become undefined. This instruction is used for both internal channel and external link communication, the transputer hardware uses the address of the channel's control word to distinguish between the two. Note that before a location can be used as a channel word for the first time, it must be initialised to *MinInt*. After the IN instruction has been executed, the channel word is automatically reset ready for further communication.

The length specified for the Input Message instruction should be the same as for the output process. For internal communications, the process which comes ready last, specifies the length of message actually transferred and so if the length output is longer, there is a possibility that the input process will be corrupted by being overwritten. For external channels, the process with the shorter message length will successfully transfer data, while the other process will hang, waiting to send or receive more data.

This instruction may take an arbitrary length of time to execute, since an arbitrarily long message may be input. Thus, it has been made interruptable in order to improve interrupt latency for high priority processes.

Example

It is desired to input a 6-byte message from the channel whose control word is located in the first word of the local workspace, and store it in a buffer which starts at the second word.

The code is split into two fragments, the first performs the initialisation of the channel word, the second the actual message input operation. We shall suppose that the local workspace starts at #F00.

opcode	mnemonic	C	B	A	[F00]
		c	b	a	–
	; initialise channel word				
24 F2	MINT	b	a	80000000	–
D0	STL 0	–	b	a	80000000
	$\vdots$				
		c	b	a	x
	; perform input from channel				
11	LDLP 1	b	a	F04	x
10	LDLP 0	a	F04	F00	x
46	LDC 6	F04	F00	6	x
F7	IN	–	–	–	80000000

At this point, there should now be six bytes stored in locations #F04 to #F09.

Note that at the start of the second code fragment, the contents of the channel word are listed as x. This is because it may either contain *MinInt* (#80000000) or a process descriptor, depending on whether the other process is ready or not.

J n   0n

Jump

$$
\begin{array}{cc}
A & \boxed{a} \\
B & \boxed{b} \\
C & \boxed{c}
\end{array}
\quad \Longrightarrow \quad
\begin{array}{c}
\boxed{-} \\
\boxed{-} \\
\boxed{-}
\end{array}
$$

$$
I \;\; \boxed{i} \quad \Longrightarrow \quad \boxed{i \,\&_{\text{byte}} n}
$$

(Note: i is the address of the following instruction.)

Note: this instruction may cause the process to be descheduled.

This instruction performs an unconditional jump to a new location specified by an offset n, to the current value of the instruction pointer, I. If the process is executing at low priority and has exceeded its time-slice, a process switch will occur after the execution of this instruction. It is for this reason that the contents of the stack have to be regarded as invalid after execution of this instruction. If it is vital that the process is not descheduled, a LDC 0 followed by a CJ should be used instead. The range of the displacement n may be extended with the positive and negative prefix instructions.

Example

Consider the high-level language instruction

```
IF WO THEN W1 := 15 ELSE W1 := -15;
```

where WO and W1 refer to the first two words in the local workspace, and where WO holds a boolean value. This instruction could be implemented using the following code, which is assumed to start at location #2000. Also, WO is assumed to hold the value *true*.

opcode	mnemonic	C	B	A	[w&1]	I
		c	*b*	*a*	–	2000
70	LDL 0	*b*	*a*	1	–	2001
A3	CJ 3	–	*b*	*a*	–	2002
4F	LDC 15	*b*	*a*	F	–	2003
D1	STL 1	–	*b*	*a*	F	2004
03	J 3	–	–	–	–	2008
60 41	LDC –15	*not executed*				
D1	STL 1	*not executed*				
; execution continues from this point						

LADD   21 F6

Long Add

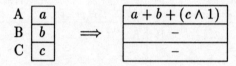

Error Flag set if an overflow occurs.

Performs the signed addition of the values in registers A and B, plus a carry in C, and places the result in register A. Overflow is checked for and sets the error flag if it occurs. This instruction implements the last stage of a multiple length addition (the first stages being implemented by the LSUM instruction), the C register containing the carry from previous stages.

Example

See LSUM for an example of long addition.

LB

F1

Load Byte

$$\begin{array}{c} A \\ B \\ C \end{array} \begin{array}{|c|} \hline a \\ \hline b \\ \hline c \\ \hline \end{array} \implies \begin{array}{|c|} \hline [a]_{\text{byte}} \\ \hline b \\ \hline c \\ \hline \end{array}$$

This instruction reads in the byte pointed to by a. Because it is a byte that is being accessed, both the word address and byte offset bits within the pointer are used (see the section on addressing for more details). The byte is loaded into the lower eight bits of A, the rest being set to zero.

Example

Suppose we wished to extract the second-from-bottom byte of the contents of A. One way of doing this would be to store this value at location 0 in the local workspace, then read back the selected byte. We shall assume that the local workspace starts at #F00, and that A initially contains #DDCCBBAA.

opcode	mnemonic	C	B	A	[w]
		c	b	DDCCBBAA	–
D0	STL 0	–	b	a	DDCCBBAA
	; load byte offset				
41	LDC 1	b	a	1	DDCCBBAA
	; load base pointer				
10	LDLP 0	a	1	F00	DDCCBBAA
	; perform indexing				
F2	BSUB	–	a	F01	DDCCBBAA
	; finally, load in the byte				
F1	LB	–	a	BB	DDCCBBAA

LDC n   4n

Load Constant

$$
\begin{array}{cc}
A \\
B \\
C
\end{array}
\begin{array}{|c|}
\hline a \\
\hline b \\
\hline c \\
\hline
\end{array}
\implies
\begin{array}{|c|}
\hline n \\
\hline a \\
\hline b \\
\hline
\end{array}
$$

Loads a constant onto the stack. The range of the constant n may be extended with the negative and positive prefix instructions.

Example

Load the values 5, 254 and −30 onto the stack.

opcode	mnemonic	C	B	A
		c	b	a
45	LDC 5	b	a	5
2F 4E	LDC 254	a	5	FE
61 42	LDC −30	5	FE	FFFFFFE2

LDIFF   24 FF

Long Difference

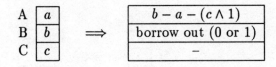

The unsigned subtraction $b - a$ is performed, with a borrow-in contained in C. The result is returned in the A register. If an overflow occurs, the borrow out returned in the B register is 1, otherwise it is 0. This instruction is designed for implementing multiple length subtraction in conjunction with the LSUB instruction.

Example

See LSUB for an example of long subtraction.

LDINF   27 F1

Load Single Length
Infinity

$$
\begin{array}{c}
\begin{array}{cc}
\text{A} & \boxed{a} \\
\text{B} & \boxed{b} \\
\text{C} & \boxed{c}
\end{array}
\quad \Longrightarrow \quad
\begin{array}{c}
\boxed{\infty_{32}} \\
\boxed{a} \\
\boxed{b}
\end{array}
\end{array}
$$

Note: this instruction is specific to the T414.

This instruction loads the A register with the bit pattern defined as positive infinity in the IEEE 754 floating point standard. It is intended for use in implementing floating point software packages for the T414.

LDIV   21 FA

Long Divide

$$
\begin{array}{c}
A \\
B \\
C
\end{array}
\begin{array}{|c|}
\hline a \\
\hline b \\
\hline c \\
\hline
\end{array}
\implies
\begin{array}{|c|}
\hline cb/a \\
\hline cb \bmod a \\
\hline - \\
\hline
\end{array}
$$

Error Flag set if $c \geq a$

Divides the double length value in the register pair CB (C containing the high word), by the single length value in register A. The unsigned dividend is returned in the A register and the remainder in the B register. Overflow (in the dividend) can occur and is checked for, the error flag being set if this occurs.

Example

Divide a double length value stored at offsets 0 (low) and 1 (high), by a single length value stored at offset 2, to produce a double length result to be stored at offsets 3 (low) and 4 (high), the single length remainder to be stored at offset 5. We shall assume that the first integer has the value #24,8300A042, the second the value 5.

opcode	mnemonic	C	B	A
	; initialise remainder	c	b	a
40	LDC 0	b	a	0
	; divide high word by divisor word			
71	LDL 1	a	0	24
72	LDL 2	0	24	5
21 FA	LDIV	–	1	7
	; store high word of result			
D4	STL 4	–	–	1
	; remainder becomes high order word for next stage			
70	LDL 0	–	1	8300A042
72	LDL 2	1	8300A042	5
21 FA	LDIV	–	3	4D668673
	; store low order word of result			
D3	STL 3	–	–	3
	; store remainder			
D5	STL 5	–	–	–

LDL n 7n

Load Local

$$
\begin{array}{c}
\text{A} \\
\text{B} \\
\text{C}
\end{array}
\begin{array}{|c|}
\hline
a \\
\hline
b \\
\hline
c \\
\hline
\end{array}
\quad\Longrightarrow\quad
\begin{array}{|c|}
\hline
[w\&n] \\
\hline
a \\
\hline
b \\
\hline
\end{array}
$$

Loads a word in the local workspace onto the stack. The instruction's operand specifies the offset within the local workspace (i.e. relative to the workspace pointer). The range of the offset n may be extended with the negative and positive prefix instructions.

Example

Load the second word of local workspace onto the stack. We assume that the local workspace starts at #F00.

opcode	mnemonic	C	B	A	[F04]
		c	b	a	x
71	LDL 1	b	a	x	x

LDLP n   1n

Load Local Pointer

A	a	$\Longrightarrow$	$w\&n$
B	b		a
C	c		b

Loads a pointer to a word in the local workspace onto the stack. The instruction's operand specifies the offset within the local workspace (i.e. relative to the workspace pointer). The range of the offset n may be extended with the negative and positive prefix instructions.

Note the similarity to the Load Local instruction: the only difference between the two is that Load Local Pointer just calculates the address of the specified word; Load Local also actually loads the word. Load Local Pointer is often used to obtain a pointer to a word for use with subsequent instructions.

Example

Load a pointer to the second word of local workspace onto the stack. We assume that the local workspace starts at #F00.

opcode	mnemonic	C	B	A
		c	b	a
11	LDLP 1	b	a	F04

LDNL n

3n

Load Non-Local

$$
\begin{array}{c}
A \\
B \\
C
\end{array}
\boxed{\begin{array}{c} a \\ b \\ c \end{array}}
\implies
\boxed{\begin{array}{c} [a\&n] \\ b \\ c \end{array}}
$$

Loads the A register with a word from memory, the address of which is specified by a pointer contained in A, indexed by the operand of the instruction. The range of the offset n, may be extended by the positive and negative prefix instructions. Note that the byte select bits of a must be zero for the instruction to be properly defined.

This instruction is usually used to load a word onto the stack from a location not contained within the local workspace. It is comparable to LDL, except that the offset is relative to A rather than to the workspace pointer. Thus it is possible for example, to evaluate an address, the result being left on the stack, then load a word relative to this address.

Example

This instruction is often used to follow static links back up a chain of workspaces in a block structured language. Conventionally, an occam process has in its local workspace, a pointer to the workspace of the lexically-enclosing process. The access of non-local variables is therefore merely a matter of following the correct number of pointers up to the lexical level of the desired variable.

We wish to access a variable (marked ⋆) two lexical levels above the current process. We shall assume that the content of the workspaces is as shown in the figure below:

process 0	process 1	process 2
		param 0
		static link 2 $\longrightarrow$
	param 2	return address
	param 1	local var 0
	param 0	local var 1 $\star$
param 1	static link 1 $\longrightarrow$	local var 2
param 0	return address	
static link 0 $\longrightarrow$	local var 0	
return address		
local var 0		
local var 1		

The code to achieve this is as follows:

opcode	mnemonic	C	B	A
		c	*b*	*a*
73	LDL 3	*b*	*a*	static link 0
32	LDNL 2	*b*	*a*	static link 1
31	LDNL 1	*b*	*a*	local var 1 $\star$

LDNLP n

5n

Load Non-Local Pointer

$$
\begin{array}{cc}
\text{A} & \boxed{a} \\
\text{B} & \boxed{b} \\
\text{C} & \boxed{c}
\end{array}
\implies
\begin{array}{c}
\boxed{a\&n} \\
\boxed{b} \\
\boxed{c}
\end{array}
$$

Loads a pointer to a word in memory. The address is specified by a pointer contained in A, indexed by the instruction's operand. The range of the offset n may be extended by the positive and negative prefix instructions. Note that the byte select bits of a must be zero for the instruction to be properly defined.

In the same way that Load Local Pointer is similar to Load Local, so Load Non-Local Pointer is similar to Load Non-Local. The only difference between the two is that Load Non-Local Pointer just calculates the address of the specified word; Load Non-Local then actually loads the word. Load Non-Local Pointer is often used to obtain a pointer to a word for use with subsequent instructions.

Example

We shall reconsider the example given for Load Non-Local. In this, we wished to obtain the value of a local variable in the workspace of a lexically-enclosing process. It is quite possible that rather than requiring the actual value of this variable, we might wish instead just to find its address. For example, if the local variable was a channel word, then we would wish to pass a pointer to it as one of the parameters of an Input Message instruction. We shall assume that the local workspace of process 2 starts at #F30.

opcode	mnemonic	C	B	A
		c	b	a
73	LDL 3	b	a	static link 0
32	LDNL 2	b	a	F30
51	LDNLP 1	b	a	F34

LDPI   21 FB

Load Pointer to Instruction

$$\begin{array}{ll} \text{A} & \boxed{a} \\ \text{B} & \boxed{b} \\ \text{C} & \boxed{c} \end{array} \implies \begin{array}{l} \boxed{i\&_{\text{byte}}a} \\ \boxed{b} \\ \boxed{c} \end{array}$$

(Note: i is the address of the following instruction.)

Returns a value in A which is the current value of the instruction pointer, indexed by a. This instruction allows the loading of the address of a location that is offset from the next instruction by the value in the A register. It has important uses in generating relocatable code.

Note that the instruction pointer points to the *next* instruction while the current instruction is being executed, so that (LDC 0; LDPI) would load a pointer to the instruction following the LDPI.

Example

The implementation of a jump table in a position independent manner requires the ability to access memory relative to the instruction pointer. We shall assume that an integer is passed in the A register indicating which routine in the jump table is required. The table contains offsets from the beginning of the table to the desired routine. We will suppose that the code starts at location #100, and that the integer in question has the value 3.

opcode	mnemonic	C	B	A	I
		c	*b*	3	100
	; load table base address				
49	LDC 9	*b*	3	9	101
21 FB	LDPI	*b*	3	10C	103
	; word offset into table				
FA	WSUB	–	*b*	118	104
	; get offset word				
30	LDNL 0	–	*b*	B0	105
	; load address of start of table				
44	LDC 4	*b*	B0	4	106
21 FB	LDPI	*b*	B0	10C	108
	; add offset to table start address				
F2	BSUB	–	*b*	1BC	109
	; transfer control				
F6	GCALL	–	*b*	10A	1BC

the table starts here at address 10C (the next word boundary after 10A).

00000080
00000090
000000A0
000000B0

LDPRI   21 FE

Load Priority

$$
\begin{array}{cc}
\text{A} & \boxed{a} \\
\text{B} & \boxed{b} \\
\text{C} & \boxed{c}
\end{array}
\implies
\begin{array}{|c|}
\hline
\text{current priority} \\
\hline
a \\
\hline
b \\
\hline
\end{array}
$$

Pushes the priority of the current process onto the stack. For the
T414, the values returned are 0 for a high priority process and 1 for a
low priority process.

Example

A process desires to construct its process descriptor. A process descriptor for the T414 consists of the workspace address with the process
priority in the least significant bit. (Remember that since the workspace
lies on a word boundary, the bottom two bits of the workspace pointer
are usually zero.) We assume that the local workspace is at location
#F00.

opcode	mnemonic	C	B	A
		c	b	a
	; get contents of workspace register			
10	LDLP 0	b	a	F00
	; load current priority			
21 FE	LDPRI	a	F00	1
	; form process descriptor			
24 FB	OR	–	a	F01

LDTIMER 22 F2

Load Timer

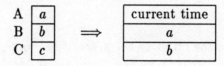

Loads the evaluation stack with the value in the current priority timer register. The timer register is incremented at regular intervals (the interval depends upon the process priority and processor speed), the value wrapping round from the most positive integer to the most negative.

Example

Suspend the current process until #2000 time units after the current time.

opcode	mnemonic	C	B	A
		c	b	a
22 20 20				
40	LDC #2000	b	a	2000
22 F2	LDTIMER	a	2000	06FDE380
25 F2	SUM	–	a	06FE0380
22 FB	TIN	–	–	–

LEND   22 F1

Loop End

Let

a = the offset to the start of the loop,
b = a pointer to the loop control block, where
$[b]$ = current loop index value,
$[b\&1]$ = current loop count.

A	a (loop offset)		−
B	b (control block adr)	$\Longrightarrow$	−
C	c		−

IF $[b\&1] > 1$ THEN

$[b\&1]$	count	$\Longrightarrow$	count − 1
$[b]$	index		index + 1

I	i	$\Longrightarrow$	$i\&_{\mathrm{byte}}(-a)$

ELSE

$[b\&1]$	count	$\Longrightarrow$	count − 1

Note: this instruction may cause the process to be descheduled.

This instruction is designed to allow easy implementation of the occam replicated constructs and the FOR loops of other languages. The B register contains the address of a pair of words. The word at offset 0 from B is the iteration variable and is incremented each time the instruction is executed. The next word up (offset 1 from B) contains a count of how many more iterations there are to go; this value is decremented each time the LEND instruction is executed. The content of the A register is subtracted from the instruction pointer if the iteration count is not zero after it is decremented. The offset is subtracted (rather than added) to facilitate the backward jumps that are normally used with this instruction, the negative prefix operation that would otherwise be necessary is eliminated.

Example

It is desired to calculate the factorial of an integer, N, initially held in the A register. The result is also to be returned in the A register. We shall solve this problem by setting up a loop that is executed N times. Each time round the loop we shall multiply a running result by the iteration variable. The iteration variable will be at offset 0 in the local workspace, the iteration count will be at offset 1, and the running result at offset 2. The local workspace starts at #F00. Since the loop is executed N times, registers and locations which change each time round the loop use we will use the variable k to represent a value from $0 \ldots k - 1$.

opcode	mnemonic	C	B	A	[F00]	[F04]	[F08]
		c	b	N	–	–	–
; set up iteration count							
D1	STL 1	–	c	b	–	N	–
; set up loop variable to 1							
41	LDC 1	c	b	1	–	N	–
D0	STL 0	–	c	b	1	N	–
; initialise running result							
41	LDC 1	c	b	1	1	N	–
D2	STL 2	–	c	b	1	N	1
	THIS IS THE START OF THE LOOP						
; Perform the multiply							
70	LDL 0	–	–	$k + 1$	$k + 1$	$N - k$	$k!$
72	LDL 2	–	$k + 1$	$k!$	$k + 1$	$N - k$	$k!$
25 F3	MUL	–	–	$(k + 1)!$	$k + 1$	$N - k$	$k!$
D2	STL 2	–	–	–	$k + 1$	$N - k$	$(k + 1)!$
; do the looping bit							
10	LDLP 0	–	–	F00	$k + 1$	$N - k$	$(k + 1)!$
49	LDC 9	–	F00	9	$k + 1$	$N - k$	$(k + 1)!$
22 F1	LEND	–	–	–	$k + 2$	$N - k - 1$	$(k + 1)!$
72	LDL 2	–	–	N!	$N + 1$	$N + 1$	N!

LMUL

23 F1

Long Multiply

$$
\begin{array}{c}
A\ \boxed{a} \\
B\ \boxed{b} \\
C\ \boxed{c}
\end{array}
\ \Longrightarrow\
\begin{array}{|c|}
\hline
\text{lo}(a \times b + c) \\
\hline
\text{hi}(a \times b + c) \\
\hline
- \\
\hline
\end{array}
$$

The LMUL instruction multiplies the two unsigned single length words contained in registers A and B and then adds the single length 'carry' contained in the C register. The result is returned in the register pair BA (high order word in B). This instruction is designed for use in implementing a multiple length multiply operation. Note that it is not possible for this instruction to cause an overflow, so the error flag is never set.

Example

Multiply the double length value #1234,5678,9ABC,DEF0, stored at offsets 1 (low) and 2 (high), by the single length value #10 stored at offset 0; storing the result at offsets 3 to 5 (low to high).

opcode	mnemonic	C	B	A
		c	b	a
; initialise carry				
40	LDC 0	b	a	0
; form low word of result				
70	LDL 0	a	0	10
71	LDL 1	0	10	9ABCDEF0
23 F1	LMUL	–	9	ABCDEF00
D3	STL 3	–	–	9
; form high words of result				
70	LDL 0	–	9	10
72	LDL 2	9	10	12345678
23 F1	LMUL	–	1	23456789
D4	STL 4	–	–	1
D5	STL 5	–	–	–

LSHL 23 F6

Long Shift Left

$$
\begin{array}{c}
A \\ B \\ C
\end{array}
\begin{array}{|c|}
\hline a \\ \hline b \\ \hline c \\ \hline
\end{array}
\implies
\begin{array}{|c|}
\hline \mathrm{lo}(cb \ll a) \\ \hline \mathrm{hi}(cb \ll a) \\ \hline - \\ \hline
\end{array}
$$

The double length value contained in the register pair CB (low word in B) is shifted left by the number of bits specified by the A register. The result is returned in the register pair BA (low word in A). If the number of places to shift is less than zero or greater than the number of bits in a double length word, the result is undefined.

Example

Single length rotation can be implemented by using the double length shift instructions. We shall rotate the contents of the A register left four bits and return the result in A.

opcode	mnemonic	C	B	A
		c	b	12345678
	; *extend to double length by clearing the upper word*			
40	LDC 0	b	12345678	0
F0	REV	b	0	12345678
	; *shift left by four places*			
44	LDC 4	0	12345678	4
23 F6	LSHL	–	1	234567890
	; *combine the two words to complete the rotation*			
24 FB	OR	–	–	234567891

LSHR 23 F5

Long Shift Right

$$
\begin{array}{ll}
A & \boxed{a} \\
B & \boxed{b} \quad \Longrightarrow \\
C & \boxed{c}
\end{array}
\quad
\begin{array}{|c|}
\hline
\text{lo}(cb \gg a) \\
\hline
\text{hi}(cb \gg a) \\
\hline
- \\
\hline
\end{array}
$$

The double length value contained in the register pair CB (low word in B) is shifted right by the number of bits specified by the A register. The result is returned in the register pair BA (low word in A). If the number of places to shift is less than zero or greater than the number of bits in a double length word, the result is undefined.

Example

The long shift right instruction can be used to implement a single length arithmetic shift (i.e. one where the sign of the number being shifted is preserved). We shall arithmetically shift the contents of the A register right by 4 bits and return the result in the A register.

opcode	mnemonic	C	B	A
		c	b	FFF1234
	; *first extend to double length*			
21 FD	XDBLE	b	FFFFFFFF	FFFF1234
	; *and then shift four places right*			
44	LDC 4	FFFFFFFF	FFFF1234	4
23 F5	LSHR	−	0FFFFFFF	FFFFF123

LSUB

23 F8

Long Subtract

$$
\begin{array}{cc}
\text{A} & \boxed{a} \\
\text{B} & \boxed{b} \\
\text{C} & \boxed{c}
\end{array}
\quad \Longrightarrow \quad
\begin{array}{|c|}
\hline
b - a - (c \wedge 1) \\
\hline
- \\
\hline
- \\
\hline
\end{array}
$$

Error flag set if arithmetic overflow occurs

Returns the result of the signed subtraction $b - a$, with a borrow-in from c. The instruction is designed to allow the implementation of multiple length subtraction in conjunction with the LDIFF instruction: LDIFF is used to subtract the (unsigned) low-order words, with LSUB used for the most significant word.

Example

It is desired to subtract the double-length signed integer stored at offsets 0 (low word) and 1 (high word) from the double-length signed integer stored at offsets 2 (low word) and 3 (high word) in the local workspace. We shall assume the first integer has the value #481234000 and the second has the value #2180021004. The result is to be placed at offsets 4 and 5.

opcode	mnemonic	C	B	A
		c	*b*	*a*
	; clear borrow			
40	LDC 0	*b*	*a*	0
	; subtract the low order words			
72	LDL 2	*a*	0	81234000
70	LDL 0	0	80021004	81234000
24 FF	LDIFF	–	1	FEDED004
	; store low order result			
D4	STL 4	–	–	1
	subtract the high order words			
73	LDL 3	–	1	21
71	LDL 1	1	21	4
23 F8	LSUB	–	–	1C
	; store high order result			
D5	STL 5	–	–	–

LSUM

23 F7

Long Sum

$$
\begin{array}{cc}
\text{A} & \boxed{a} \\
\text{B} & \boxed{b} \\
\text{C} & \boxed{c}
\end{array}
\quad\Longrightarrow\quad
\begin{array}{|c|}
\hline
a + b + (c \wedge 1) \\
\hline
\text{carry out} \\
\hline
- \\
\hline
\end{array}
$$

Performs the unsigned addition of the values in the registers A and B plus a carry-in in C and places the result in register A with a carry-out in B (0 or 1). The instruction is designed to allow the implementation of multiple length addition in conjunction with the LADD instruction: LSUM is used to add the (unsigned) low-order words, with LADD used for the most significant word.

Example

It is desired to add together two double length signed integers contained in the local workspace. The first integer is stored at offsets 0 (low word) and 1 (high word) and has the value #481234000, the second at offsets 2 (low word) and 3 (high word) and has the value #2180021004. The result is to be placed at offsets 4 and 5.

opcode	mnemonic	C	B	A
		c	*b*	*a*
	; clear carry			
40	LDC 0	*b*	*a*	0
	; add the low order words			
70	LDL 0	*a*	0	81234000
72	LDL 2	0	81234000	80021004
23 F7	LSUM	–	1	01255004
	; store low order result			
D4	STL 4	–	–	1
	; add the high order words			
71	LDL 1	–	1	4
73	LDL 3	1	4	21
21 F6	LADD	–	–	26
	; store high order result			
D5	STL 5	–	–	–

MINT   24 F2

Minimum Integer

$$
\begin{array}{cc}
\text{A} & \boxed{a} \\
\text{B} & \boxed{b} \\
\text{C} & \boxed{c}
\end{array}
\implies
\begin{array}{c}
\boxed{\begin{array}{c} MinInt \\ a \\ b \end{array}}
\end{array}
$$

Pushes the most negative representable integer onto the stack. For the T414 this has the value of #80000000. This instruction avoids the use of a load constant instruction that would otherwise need seven prefix instructions. It also loads the minimum integer in a manner independent of processor word length, which is useful for the special flag uses indicated in the next paragraph.

The minimum integer is used by various transputer instructions. A channel control word is set to *MinInt* to indicate that no process is ready to communicate on that channel. The process queue registers contain *MinInt* when there is no process on the queue. Similarly, *MinInt* is used to indicate the end of a timer queue, either in a timer queue register if the queue is empty, or in the timer chain pointer of a queued workspace. These and other uses are described in detail elsewhere in this book.

Example

Reserve space for, and initialise, a channel control word. We assume that the local workspace is at location #F00.

opcode	mnemonic	C	B	A	W	[w]
		c	b	a	F00	–
60 BF	AJW -1	c	b	a	EFC	–
24 F2	MINT	b	a	80000000	EFC	–
D0	STL 0	–	b	a	EFC	80000000

MOVE **24 FA**

Move Message

Let

a = number of bytes to transfer,
b = destination start address,
c = source start address.

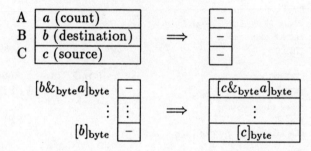

The block of memory starting from the address in the C register, of length specified by the A register, is copied to the block of memory starting from the address in the B register. The two blocks of memory must not overlap.

This instruction may take an arbitrary length of time to execute, since an arbitrarily long block of data may be moved. Thus, it has been made interruptable in order to improve interrupt latency for high priority processes.

Example

This instruction may obviously be used to implement vector (or equivalent) assignments, but a less obvious use is in extracting 16-bit (or any integral byte length) fields from memory. For instance, consider the problem of adding a constant (5 say) to the fourth element in an INT16 array starting at word offset 7 in the local workspace. We shall use offset 0 as a scratch location. We assume that the local workspace is at location #F00.

opcode	mnemonic	C	B	A
		c	*b*	*a*
	; *initialise scratch location*			
40	LDC 0	*b*	*a*	0
D0	STL 0	–	*b*	*a*
	; *load 2× array index*			
46	LDC 6	*b*	*a*	6
	; *load array base address*			
17	LDLP 7	*a*	6	F1C
	; *index into INT16 array*			
F2	BSUB	–	*a*	F22
	; *move desired INT16 to scratch location*			
10	LDLP 0	*a*	F22	F00
42	LDC 2	F22	F00	2
24 FA	MOVE	–	–	–
	; *load desired INT16 and extend to word*			
70	LDL 0	–	–	0000FF36
28 20 20				
40	LDC #8000	–	0000FF36	00008000
23 FA	XWORD	–	–	FFFFFF36
	; *add the constant*			
85	ADC 5	–	–	FFFFFF31
	; *check still in INT16 range*			
28 20 20				
40	LDC #8000	–	FFFFFF31	00008000
25 F6	CWORD	–	–	FFFFFF31
	; *store back in scratch location*			
D0	STL 0	–	–	–
	; *get source address for move*			
10	LDLP 0	–	–	F00
	; *calculate array address again*			
46	LDC 6	–	F00	6
17	LDLP 7	F00	6	F1C
F2	BSUB	–	F00	F22
	; *move INT16 back into array*			
42	LDC 2	F00	F22	2
24 FA	MOVE	–	–	–

MUL   25 F3

Multiply

$$
\begin{array}{cc}
\text{A} & \boxed{a} \\
\text{B} & \boxed{b} \\
\text{C} & \boxed{c}
\end{array}
\quad \Longrightarrow \quad
\begin{array}{c}
\boxed{a \times b} \\
\boxed{c} \\
\boxed{-}
\end{array}
$$

Error flag set on arithmetic overflow.

Multiplies the signed integers contained in A and B and returns the signed result in A. The error flag is set if an arithmetic overflow occurs.

Example

If the values in the registers A and B are #32 and #5 respectively then the value in the A register will be #FA after the multiply operation.

opcode	mnemonic	C	B	A
		c	b	a
23 42	LDC #32	b	a	32
45	LDC 5	a	32	5
25 F3	MUL	$-$	a	FA

NFIX n   6n

Negative Prefix

Not strictly speaking an instruction; this operator is used in conjunction with PFIX (Prefix) to extend the range of the operands of those thirteen instructions which use operands.

Each transputer instruction byte has a four-bit operator field and a four-bit operand field. When each byte is executed, the four operand bits are shifted left into a special operand register. The contents of the operand register are then used as the operand for the instruction. Normally, the operand register is cleared after each instruction has been executed; PFIX and NFIX are special in that they do not clear this register after execution, allowing operands larger than four bits to be built up. For example, to load the constant #123, the sequence PFIX 1; PFIX 2; LDC 3 would be used. Normally however, we would not consider PFIX as an instruction in its own right, and would refer directly to LDC #123, leaving the assembler to insert prefix instructions as necessary.

NFIX works in exactly the same way as PFIX, except that it complements the operand register after shifting; this allows negative operands to be built up quickly. For example, LDC -2 is equivalent to NFIX 0; LDC #E. The NFIX 0 loads zero into the operand register; this is then complemented, leaving #FFFFFFFF or −1. The value #E is then shifted left into the register, leaving a final value of #FFFFFFFE or −2.

NORM   21 F9

Normalise

Let

k = number of leading zeroes in the double-length
word *ba*.

A	a
B	b
C	c

$\Longrightarrow$

$lo(ba \ll k)$
$hi(ba \ll k)$
k

The normalise instruction shifts the double length value in the register pair BA (low order word in A) until the most significant bit is a one. The number of places shifted is returned in the C register and the shifted value is left in the BA register pair. If the initial value is zero, a value equal to twice the word length is returned in C, (64 in the case of the T414).

This instruction only provides a normalise operation for positive values. To implement a normalise for a negative value, it is necessary to complement the value before and after the normalise instruction.

Example

Normalise the double length value contained at offsets 0 (low order word) and 1 in the local workspace. This code fragment assumes the double length value is positive.

opcode	mnemonic	C	B	A
		c	b	a
71	LDL 1	b	a	00000024
70	LDL 0	a	00000024	3100042F
21 F9	NORM	1A	90C40010	BC000000

NOT 23 F2

Bitwise Complement

$$
\begin{array}{c}
A \\ B \\ C
\end{array}
\boxed{\begin{array}{c} a \\ b \\ c \end{array}}
\implies
\boxed{\begin{array}{c} \sim a \\ b \\ c \end{array}}
$$

Returns the (one's) complement of the value at the top of the stack; that is to say, it inverts every bit in the A register.

Example

Find the complement of #C2

opcode	mnemonic	C	B	A
		c	b	a
2C 42	LDC #C2	b	a	C2
23 F2	NOT	b	a	FFFFFF3D

OPR n   Fn

Operate

Not strictly speaking an instruction; this operator is used to extend the number of instructions available to the transputer. Since each transputer instruction byte is divided into a four-bit operator field and a four-bit operand field, this allows for a maximum of sixteen instructions, (or fourteen once the Prefix and Negative Prefix instructions are taken into consideration). Operate provides a way out: it interprets its operand as an opcode, allowing access to a further sixteen instructions, or in conjunction with Prefix, a potentially unlimited number. The only drawback with this method is that the extra instructions do not have operands; in general however, they get round this by using implicitly defined operands; for example the OR instruction uses the values in the A and B registers as its operands.

Normally we would not consider OPR as an instruction in its own right. For example, OR has the instruction number #4B, so the sequence PFIX 4; OPR #B would execute the OR instruction. However, we would normally just tell the assembler 'OR' and expect it to produce the two opcodes 24 and FB directly.

Note that throughout this book, we give the opcodes required to execute an instruction, rather than the instruction number. For example, on the next page OR is referred to as having opcode '24 FB', rather than instruction number 4B.

OR 24 FB

Bitwise OR

$$
\begin{array}{cc}
\text{A} & \boxed{a} \\
\text{B} & \boxed{b} \\
\text{C} & \boxed{c}
\end{array}
\implies
\begin{array}{c}
\boxed{a \vee b} \\
\boxed{c} \\
\boxed{-}
\end{array}
$$

Performs a bitwise OR between the top two operands on the stack.

Example

Perform an bitwise OR between #C2 and #AB.

opcode	mnemonic	C	B	A
		c	b	a
2C 42	LDC #C2	b	a	C2
2A 4B	LDC #AB	a	C2	AB
24 FB	OR	–	a	EB

OUT FB

Output Message

Let

a = the number of bytes to transfer,
b = the channel address,
c = the source start address.

A	a (count)
B	b (channel)
C	c (source)

$\Longrightarrow$

–
–
–

Note: this instruction may cause the process to be descheduled.

Outputs the number of words specified by the value in the A register to a channel which is pointed to by the B register, starting from the memory location pointed to by the C register. (See also **IN**.) All three registers are left undefined. This instruction is used for both internal channel and external link communication, the transputer hardware uses the address of the channel's control word to distinguish the two.

The microcode for this instruction is in fact rather complex, based on the fact that the process waiting on the other end of the channel may either be doing an **Input Message**, or an **ALT**. A full description of what this instruction does is as follows:

Let $chan = [b]$

IF $chan = MinInt$
THEN other process has not begun communicating:

$chan$ $\boxed{MinInt}$ $\Longrightarrow$ $\boxed{w}$

$[w\&{-}1]$ $\boxed{-}$ $\Longrightarrow$ $\boxed{i}$

$$[w\&-3]\ \boxed{-}\quad \Longrightarrow \quad \boxed{c}$$

and the process is descheduled.

IF $chan \neq MinInt$ AND $[chan\& - 3] = MinInt + 1$
THEN other process is an ALT which has not yet reached
the **ALTWT**:

$$[chan\& - 3]\ \boxed{MinInt+1}\quad \Longrightarrow \quad \boxed{MinInt+3}$$

$$chan\ \boxed{-}\quad \Longrightarrow \quad \boxed{w}$$

$$[w\&-1]\ \boxed{-}\quad \Longrightarrow \quad \boxed{i}$$

$$[w\&-3]\ \boxed{-}\quad \Longrightarrow \quad \boxed{c}$$

and the process is descheduled.

IF $chan \neq MinInt$ AND $[chan\& - 3] = MinInt + 2$
THEN other process is an ALT which has descheduled after
reaching the **ALTWT**:

$$[chan\& - 3]\ \boxed{MinInt+2}\quad \Longrightarrow \quad \boxed{MinInt+3}$$

$$chan\ \boxed{-}\quad \Longrightarrow \quad \boxed{w}$$

$$[w\&-1]\ \boxed{-}\quad \Longrightarrow \quad \boxed{i}$$

$$[w\&-3]\ \boxed{-}\quad \Longrightarrow \quad \boxed{c}$$

ALT process is rescheduled, and this process is descheduled.

IF $chan \neq MinInt$ AND $[chan\& - 3] = MinInt + 3$
THEN other process is an ALT which has already fired on
another channel (or time), so behave like the first-arriving
process in a normal communication:

$$chan\ \boxed{-}\quad \Longrightarrow \quad \boxed{w}$$

$$[w\&-1]\ \boxed{-}\quad \Longrightarrow \quad \boxed{i}$$

$$[w\&-3]\ \boxed{-}\quad \Longrightarrow \quad \boxed{c}$$

and the process is descheduled.

ELSE other process is an ordinary Input Message waiting to communicate:

transfer a bytes from $[c]$ onwards to $[chan\& - 3]$ onwards; and reschedule the other process.

This instruction may take an arbitrary length of time to execute, since an arbitrarily long message may be output. Thus, it has been made interruptable in order to improve interrupt latency for high priority processes.

Example

It is desired to output a 20-byte message from the channel whose control word is located in the local workspace. The code is split into two fragments: the first represents the declaration of the channel in the local workspace, the second the actual message output operation. It is assumed that there are no further local declarations after the channel declaration so that in the second fragment, the channel's control word is at offset 0 in the local workspace. The message to be output starts at offset 1 in the local workspace. We assume that the local workspace is at location #F00.

opcode	mnemonic	C	B	A	W	[w]
		c	b	a	F00	–
; reserve space for channel and initialise						
60 BF	AJW -1	c	b	a	EFC	–
24 F2	MINT	b	a	80000000	EFC	–
D0	STL 0	–	b	a	EFC	80000000
; output a message on the channel						
		c	b	a	EFC	x
21 44	LDC 20	b	a	14	EFC	x
10	LDLP 0	a	14	EFC	EFC	x
11	LDLP 1	14	EFC	F00	EFC	x
FB	OUT	–	–	–	EFC	80000000

Note that in the second half of this example, we have used x to represent the contents of the channel word, since this may hold either *MinInt* or a process descriptor, depending upon whether the other communicating process is ready. Note also that the channel word is automatically reinitialised ready for further communication.

OUTBYTE   FE

Output Byte

Let

a = the value of the byte to transfer,
b = the channel address.

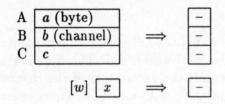

Note: this instruction may cause the process to be descheduled.

Outputs the byte contained in the register A to the channel whose control word is pointed to by the B register. No input byte instruction is provided, so the corresponding input has to be implemented by an **Input Message** instruction with a length of one. Offset 0 in the local workspace is used and corrupted by this instruction. All three registers are also left undefined. This instruction is used for both internal channel and external link communication; the transputer hardware uses the address of the channel's control word to distinguish between the two.

Note that this instruction works by storing the data value at local 0, and then performing the equivalent of an **Output Message**, with a pointer to local 0. See **OUT** for a more detailed explanation of how message outputting works.

Example

It is desired to output the byte constant #20 on the channel whose control word is located in the local workspace. The code is split into two fragments, the first represents the declaration of the channel in the local workspace, the second the actual byte output operation. It is assumed that there are no further local declarations after the channel declaration so that in the second fragment the channel's control word is initially at offset 0 in the local workspace. Note that when actually outputting from the channel, we reserve an extra location in the workspace since offset 0 becomes corrupted. We assume that the local workspace is at location #F00.

opcode	mnemonic	C	B	A	W	[EFC]
		c	*b*	*a*	F00	–
; reserve space for channel and initialise						
60 BF	AJW -1	*c*	*b*	*a*	EFC	–
24 F2	MINT	*b*	*a*	80000000	EFC	–
D0	STL 0	–	*b*	*a*	EFC	80000000
; output a message on the channel						
		c	*b*	*a*	EFC	*x*
; reserve extra location						
60 BF	AJW -1	*c*	*b*	*a*	EF8	*x*
10	LDLP 1	*b*	*a*	EFC	EF8	*x*
21 44	LDC #20	*a*	EFC	20	EF8	*x*
FE	OUTBYTE	–	–	–	EF8	80000000
B1	AJW 1	–	–	–	EFC	80000000

Note that in the second half of this example, we have used x to represent the contents of the channel word, since this may hold either *MinInt* or a process descriptor, depending upon whether the other communicating process is ready. Note also that the channel word is automatically reinitialised ready for further communication.

OUTWORD   FF

Output Word

Let

a = the value of the word to transfer,
b = the channel address.

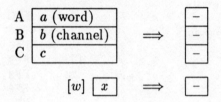

Note: this instruction may cause the process to be descheduled.

Outputs the word contained in the A register to the channel whose
control word is pointed to by the B register. No input word instruction is
provided, so the corresponding input has to be implemented by an **Input
Message** instruction with a length of four. Offset 0 in the local workspace
is used and corrupted by this instruction. All three registers are also
left undefined. This instruction is used for both internal channel and
external link communication; the transputer hardware uses the address
of the channel's control word to distinguish between the two.

Note that this instruction works by storing the data value at local
0, and then performing the equivalent of an **Output Message**, with a
pointer to local 0. See **OUT** for a more detailed explanation of how
message outputting works.

Example

It is desired to output the word constant #F20 on the channel whose
control word is located in the local workspace. The code is split into two
fragments: the first represents the declaration of the channel in the local
workspace, the second the actual word output operation. It is assumed
that there are no further local declarations after the channel declaration

so that in the second fragment the channel's control word is at offset 0 in the local workspace. Note that when actually outputting from the channel, we reserve an extra location in the workspace since offset 0 becomes corrupted. We assume that the local workspace is at location #F00.

opcode	mnemonic	C	B	A	W	[EFC]
		c	b	a	F00	–
; reserve space for channel and initialise						
60 BF	AJW -1	c	b	a	EFC	–
24 F2	MINT	b	a	80000000	EFC	–
D0	STL 0	–	b	a	EFC	80000000
; output a message on the channel						
		c	b	a	EFC	x
	; reserve extra location					
60 BF	AJW -1	c	b	a	EF8	x
10	LDLP 1	b	a	EFC	EF8	x
2F 21 44	LDC #F20	a	EFC	F20	EF8	x
FF	OUTWORD	–	–	–	EF8	80000000
B1	AJW 1	–	–	–	EFC	80000000

Note that in the second half of this example, we have used x to represent the contents of the channel word, since this may hold either *MinInt* or a process descriptor, depending upon whether the other communicating process is ready. Note also that the channel word is automatically reinitialised ready for further communication.

PFIX n   2n

Prefix

Not strictly speaking an instruction; this operator is used in conjunction with NFIX (Negative Prefix) to extend the range of the operands of those thirteen instructions which use operands.

Each transputer instruction byte has a four-bit operator field and a four-bit operand field. When each byte is executed, the four operand bits are shifted left into a special operand register. The contents of the operand register are then used as the operand for the instruction. Normally, the operand register is cleared after each instruction has been executed; PFIX and NFIX are special in that they do not clear this register after execution, allowing operands larger than four bits to be built up. For example, to load the constant #123, the sequence PFIX 1; PFIX 2; LDC 3 would be used. Normally however, we would not consider PFIX as an instruction in its own right, and would refer directly to LDC #123, leaving the assembler to insert prefix instructions as necessary.

NFIX works in exactly the same way as PFIX, except that it complements the operand register after shifting; this allows negative operands to be built up quickly. For example, LDC -2 is equivalent to NFIX 0; LDC #E.

POSTNORMSN 26 FC

Post-Normalise Correction

Let

a = the guard word,
b = the normalised fraction,
c = the normalising shift length,
e = the exponent.

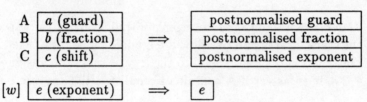

A	a (guard)			postnormalised guard
B	b (fraction)	$\Longrightarrow$		postnormalised fraction
C	c (shift)			postnormalised exponent

$[w]$ | e (exponent) | $\Longrightarrow$ | e

Note: this instruction is specific to the T414.

This instruction performs a postnormalise correction on a single length floating point number. It is intended for use in implementing floating point software packages for the T414.

PROD   F8

Unsigned Multiplication (Product)

$$
\begin{array}{c|c}
A & a \\
B & b \\
C & c
\end{array}
\quad\Longrightarrow\quad
\begin{array}{|c|}
\hline
a \times_{\text{unsigned}} b \\
\hline
c \\
\hline
- \\
\hline
\end{array}
$$

Calculates the unsigned integer multiplication of the top two values on the stack. Carry and overflow are ignored. The time taken to execute this instruction is proportional to the logarithm of the unsigned contents of A, i.e. it is fastest if A contains a small positive integer.

Example

This instruction is useful for evaluating multidimensional array subscripts. Consider the array defined in occam as:

    [9][4][7]INT Fred:

To generate the address of array element `Fred[p][q][r]` requires the following code, ignoring array bound checking and assuming that the variables p,q and r are at offsets 0, 1 and 2 respectively in the local workspace, and that the array Fred starts at offset 3. Note that the code is arranged so that the smallest number is always loaded as the second operand to the PROD. We assume that the local workspace is at location #F00, and that the variables p,q and r have the values 3,2 and 6 respectively.

opcode	mnemonic	C	B	A
		c	*b*	*a*
44	LDC 4	*b*	*a*	4
70	LDL 0	*a*	4	3
F8	PROD	–	*a*	C
71	LDL 1	*a*	C	2
F5	ADD	–	*a*	E
47	LDC 7	*a*	E	7
F8	PROD	–	*a*	62
72	LDL 2	*a*	62	6
F5	ADD	–	*a*	68
13	LDLP 3	*a*	68	F0C
FA	WSUB	–	*a*	10AC

REM   21 FF

Remainder

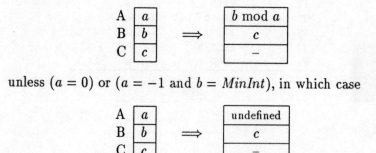

unless $(a = 0)$ or $(a = -1$ and $b = MinInt)$, in which case

Returns the remainder of the division of the top two values on the stack. This function is also known by the name 'modulus'. The sign of the remainder is the same as the sign of the quotient. See also DIV.

Example

Find the remainder of the division of 42 by 11.

opcode	mnemonic	C	B	A
		c	b	a
22 4A	LDC 42	b	a	2A
4B	LDC 11	a	2A	B
21 FF	REM	–	a	9

RESETCH   21 F2

Reset Channel

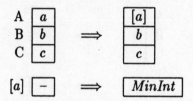

The contents of the channel control word pointed to by the A register is returned on the stack. The control word is set to *MinInt*. If the control word pointed to is that of a hardware link, the link hardware is also reset. If the returned contents of the control word are not *MinInt*, indicating that a process was waiting on the channel, then that process may be rescheduled with a RUNP instruction, since the value in A will be a process descriptor.

This instruction is intimately involved with the transputer hardware and should only be used in situations where a communications failure cannot be tolerated. For further information see the INMOS technical note 'Extraordinary use of Transputer Links' [5].

RET   22 F0

Return

$$
\begin{array}{cc}
A & \boxed{a} \\
B & \boxed{b} \quad \Longrightarrow \\
C & \boxed{c}
\end{array}
\qquad
\begin{array}{c}
\boxed{a} \\
\boxed{b} \\
\boxed{c}
\end{array}
$$

$$
I \ \boxed{i} \quad \Longrightarrow \quad \boxed{[w]}
$$

$$
W \ \boxed{w} \quad \Longrightarrow \quad \boxed{w\&4}
$$

(Note: i is the address of the following instruction.)

The **Return** instruction loads the instruction pointer with the return address and releases the four workspace locations that were reserved by the **Call** instruction. The three evaluation stack registers are not affected, so up to three values may be returned through them.

Example

Return from a subroutine called from location #A0, so the return address is #A1. We assume that the local workspace is at location #F00.

opcode	mnemonic	C	B	A	W	[w]	I
		c	b	a	F00	A1	–
22 F0	RET	c	b	a	F10	–	A1

REV   F0

Reverse

$$
\begin{array}{cc}
A & \boxed{a} \\
B & \boxed{b} \\
C & \boxed{c}
\end{array}
\quad\Longrightarrow\quad
\begin{array}{c}
\boxed{b} \\
\boxed{a} \\
\boxed{c}
\end{array}
$$

Exchanges the values in the registers A and B. All other registers are unaffected. This instruction is very useful for relaxing the order in which expressions, array subscripts and the like may be evaluated.

Example

If A contains the value #C2 and B contains the value #AB, then after this instruction the value in A will become #AB and the value in B will become #C2.

opcode	mnemonic	C	B	A
		c	b	a
2C 42	LDC #C2	b	a	C2
2A 4B	LDC #AB	a	C2	AB
F0	REV	a	AB	C2

ROUNDSN   26 FD

Round Single Length
Floating Point Number

Let

a = the guard word,
b = the fractional part,
c = the exponent.

A	a (guard)		result
B	b (fraction)	$\Longrightarrow$	–
C	c (exponent)		–

Note: this instruction is specific to the T414.

Rounds a floating point number and packs its exponent and mantissa into a single word. Rounding is performed in 'Round to Nearest' mode as defined in IEEE 754. This instruction is intended for use in implementing floating point software packages for the T414.

RUNP 23 F9

Run Process

Let

a = the descriptor of the process to be scheduled.

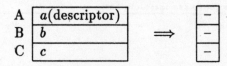

Adds the process whose descriptor is passed in the A register to the appropriate process queue. A process descriptor consists of a pointer to the workspace of the process OR'ed with the priority of the process. For the T414, the priority of the process (0 or 1) is therefore contained in the bottom bit and the workspace pointer in the top 30 bits. The address to begin execution at is assumed to have been already stored at the location immediately below the workspace (i.e. $[w\&-1]$) of the new process. This instruction allows the scheduling of processes at any level of priority, unlike the STARTP instruction that schedules a process at the current priority.

Example

Schedule a process whose workspace is located at address #1000 on the low priority (priority bit = 1) queue. Execution is to begin at offset #40 from the RUNP instruction. We will assume that the code fragment starts at address #200.

opcode	mnemonic	C	B	A	I
		c	b	a	200
	; set up start address at location −1			–	
24 4A	LDC #40+10	b	a	4A	202
21 FB	LDPI	b	a	24E	204
21 20 20					
40	LDC #1000	a	24E	1000	208
60 EF	STNL −1	–	–	a	20A
	; load descriptor				
21 20 20					
40	LDC #1000	–	a	1001	20E
	; run process				
23 F9	RUNP	–	–	–	210
	; this process continues execution here				

SAVEH

23 FE

Save High Priority Queue Registers

$$
\begin{array}{cc}
A & \boxed{a} \\
B & \boxed{b} \\
C & \boxed{c}
\end{array}
\quad\Longrightarrow\quad
\begin{array}{c}
\boxed{b} \\
\boxed{c} \\
\boxed{-}
\end{array}
$$

$$
\begin{array}{cc}
[a\&1] & \boxed{-} \\
[a] & \boxed{-}
\end{array}
\quad\Longrightarrow\quad
\begin{array}{|l|}
\hline
\textit{High Priority Back Pointer} \\
\hline
\textit{High Priority Front Pointer} \\
\hline
\end{array}
$$

The contents of the high priority queue registers are copied to memory, the front pointer at the location pointed to by the A register and the back pointer at the next word up. If there are no entries in the queue both these registers will contain *MinInt*. The main purpose of this instruction (and its sister instruction SAVEL) is for debugging, allowing the contents of the high priority queue to be inspected.

Example

The contents of the high priority queue registers are to be stored at offsets 5 and 6 in the local workspace. We assume that the local workspace is at location #F00.

opcode	mnemonic	C	B	A	[w&5]	[w&6]
		c	b	a	–	–
15	LDLP 5	b	a	F14	–	–
23 FE	SAVEH	–	b	a	FrontP	BackP

SAVEL   23 FD

Save Low Priority Queue Registers

$$
\begin{array}{cc}
A & \boxed{a} \\
B & \boxed{b} \\
C & \boxed{c}
\end{array}
\implies
\begin{array}{c}
\boxed{b} \\
\boxed{c} \\
\boxed{-}
\end{array}
$$

$$
\begin{array}{cc}
[a\&1] & \boxed{-} \\
[a] & \boxed{-}
\end{array}
\implies
\begin{array}{|l|}
\hline
\textit{Low Priority Back Pointer} \\
\hline
\textit{Low Priority Front Pointer} \\
\hline
\end{array}
$$

The contents of the low priority queue registers are copied to memory, the front pointer at the location pointed to by the A register and the back pointer at the next word up. If there are no entries in the queue both these registers will contain *MinInt*. The main purpose of this instruction (and its sister instruction SAVEH) is for debugging, allowing the contents of the low priority queue to be inspected.

Example

The contents of the low priority queue registers are to be stored at offsets 5 and 6 in the local workspace. We assume that the local workspace is at location #F00.

opcode	mnemonic	C	B	A	[w&5]	[w&6]
		c	b	a	–	–
15	LDLP 5	b	a	F14	–	–
23 FD	SAVEL	–	b	a	FrontP	BackP

SB

23 FB

Store Byte

$$
\begin{array}{ccc}
\text{A} & \boxed{a} & & \boxed{c} \\
\text{B} & \boxed{b} & \Longrightarrow & \boxed{-} \\
\text{C} & \boxed{c} & & \boxed{-}
\end{array}
$$

$$
[a]_{\text{byte}} \ \boxed{-} \quad \Longrightarrow \quad \boxed{b \wedge 255}
$$

Stores a byte in memory. The address is specified in A, and the value to be stored is in the lower 8 bits of B. This is one of the few instructions where the byte select bits of the address are used. Note that this instruction executes using a single write cycle; this is because the transputer has external circuitry which allows it to write to a selected byte within a word of memory, avoiding a read-modify-write sequence.

Example

Store #FF at location #3F1—i.e. the second byte of the word at location #3F0.

opcode	mnemonic	C	B	A	[#3F0]
		c	b	a	xxxxxxxx
2F 4F	LDC #FF	b	a	FF	xxxxxxxx
23 2F 41	LDC #3F1	a	FF	3F1	xxxxxxxx
23 FB	SB	–	–	a	xxxxFFxx

SETERR   21 F0

Set Error

$$
\begin{array}{cc}
\begin{array}{cc}
A & \boxed{a} \\
B & \boxed{b} \\
C & \boxed{c}
\end{array}
&
\Longrightarrow
&
\begin{array}{c}
\boxed{a} \\
\boxed{b} \\
\boxed{c}
\end{array}
\end{array}
$$

$$
\textit{Error Flag}\ \ \boxed{-}\ \ \Longrightarrow\ \ \boxed{\textit{true}}
$$

Sets the error flag. Subsequent operation of the transputer then depends on the state of the Halt-On-Error flag (see **Set Halt-on-Error Flag**).

SETHALTERR   25 F8

Set Halt-on-Error Flag

$$
\begin{array}{cc}
A & \boxed{a} \\
B & \boxed{b} \\
C & \boxed{c}
\end{array}
\implies
\begin{array}{c}
\boxed{a} \\
\boxed{b} \\
\boxed{c}
\end{array}
$$

Halt-on-Error Flag $\boxed{-}$ $\implies$ $\boxed{true}$

The halt-on-error flag is set. This puts the transputer into the mode in which the processor stops if the error flag becomes set.

SHL   24 F1

Shift Left

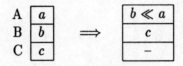

Shifts the value in B left a places, filling the bits created with zeroes, and returns the result in A. The effect is undefined if A contains a value larger than the number of bits in a word. The time taken to execute this instruction is proportional to the unsigned contents of A, so attempts to shift by large values (or small negative values) may lock the processor up for considerable periods of time.

Example

Shift left the value #AB by two places.

opcode	mnemonic	C	B	A
		c	b	a
2A 4B	LDC #AB	b	a	AB
42	LDC 2	a	AB	2
24 F1	SHL	–	a	2AC

SHR

24 F0

Shift Right

A	a		$b \gg a$
B	b	$\Longrightarrow$	c
C	c		–

Shifts the value in B right a places, filling the bits created with zeros, and returns the result in A. The effect is undefined if A contains a value larger than the number of bits in a word. The time taken to execute this instruction is proportional to the unsigned contents of A, so attempts to shift by large values (or small negative values) may lock the processor up for considerable periods of time.

Example

Shift right the value #AB by two places.

opcode	mnemonic	C	B	A
		c	b	a
2A 4B	LDC #AB	b	a	AB
42	LDC 2	a	AB	2
24 F0	SHR	–	a	2A

STARTP   **FD**

Start Process

Let

a = the address of the new workspace,
b = the offset from I to the start of the process.

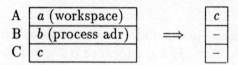

This instruction schedules a new process, that is to say, it adds a process to the rear of the appropriate active process queue. The current process continues unaffected. The initial execution address for the new process is given by the value in B as an offset from the instruction pointer I. The value of I used is that after the instruction has executed, i.e. the offset is relative to the instruction following the **STARTP**. The A register specifies the address of the workspace. See **ENDP** for details of stopping child processes and keeping track of the number of children left executing. The process is scheduled at the same priority level as the creating process

Example

A piece of code executing at #A0 desires to start two daughter processes, one at #B0 and one at #C0, giving the first a workspace at #F10, the second at #F20. The current workspace is at #F00. We assume that space for the child process count has already been reserved.

opcode	mnemonic	C	B	A	I	[F00]
		c	*b*	*a*	A0	–
	; *first set up child process count*					
42	LDC 2	*b*	*a*	A1		–
D0	STL 0	–	*b*	*a*	A2	2
	; *next start first child*					
4A	LDC #A	*b*	*a*	A	A3	2
21 10	LDLP #10	*a*	A	F10	A5	2
FD	STARTP	–	–	*a*	A6	2
	; *start the second child*					
21 45	LDC #15	–	*a*	15	A8	2
21 20	LDLP #20	*a*	15	F20	AA	2
FD	STARTP	–	–	*a*	AB	2

STHB   25 F0

Store High Priority Back Pointer

$$
\begin{array}{ccc}
\begin{array}{cc} A & \boxed{a} \\ B & \boxed{b} \\ C & \boxed{c} \end{array} & \Longrightarrow & \begin{array}{c} \boxed{b} \\ \boxed{c} \\ \boxed{-} \end{array}
\end{array}
$$

$$
\textit{High Priority Back Ptr } \boxed{-} \quad \Longrightarrow \quad \boxed{a}
$$

Puts the contents of the A register into the high priority back pointer register. This instruction should not be used for manipulating the contents of the process queue because no interlock mechanism is provided to prevent the processor accessing the queue while a user program is in the middle of modifying them. During booting, it is not, in fact, necessary to initialise the back pointers since the transputer can detect the special case of no active processes (front pointer = *MinInt*) and take appropriate action.

Note: this instruction is different from Save High Priority Queue Registers, which writes the current values of those registers to memory.

STHF

21 F8

Store High Priority Front Pointer

$$\begin{array}{c} A \\ B \\ C \end{array} \boxed{\begin{array}{c} a \\ b \\ c \end{array}} \implies \boxed{\begin{array}{c} b \\ c \\ - \end{array}}$$

High Priority Front Ptr $\boxed{-}$ $\implies$ $\boxed{a}$

Puts the contents of the A register into the high priority front pointer register. This instruction should only be used for initialising the high priority process queue. It should not be used for manipulating the contents of the process queue, because no interlock mechanism is provided to prevent the processor accessing the queue while a user program is in the middle of modifying them.

Note: this instruction is different from Save High Priority Queue Registers, which writes the current values of those registers to memory.

Example

Initialise the high priority process queue. This must be done after a reset and before any scheduling operations can be done.

opcode	mnemonic	C	B	A
		c	*b*	*a*
	; initialise front pointer			
24 F2	MINT	*b*	*a*	80000000
21 F8	STHF	–	*b*	*a*

STL n   Dn

Store Local

$$
\begin{array}{cc}
\begin{array}{c}
A \\ B \\ C
\end{array}
\begin{array}{|c|}
\hline a \\ \hline b \\ \hline c \\ \hline
\end{array}
& \Longrightarrow
\begin{array}{|c|}
\hline b \\ \hline c \\ \hline - \\ \hline
\end{array}
\end{array}
$$

$$
[w\&n] \begin{array}{|c|} \hline - \\ \hline \end{array} \Longrightarrow \begin{array}{|c|} \hline a \\ \hline \end{array}
$$

Stores the word at the top of the evaluation stack in the local work-space (c.f. LDL). The instruction's operand specifies the offset within the local workspace (i.e. relative to the workspace pointer) where the word is to be stored. The range of the offset n may be extended with the negative and positive prefix instructions.

Example

Store #8E7 in the second word of local workspace. We assume that the local workspace is at location #F00.

opcode	mnemonic	C	B	A	[#F04]
		c	b	a	-
28 2E 47	LDC #8E7	b	a	8E7	-
D1	STL 1	-	b	a	8E7

STLB

21 F7

Store Low Priority Back
Pointer

$$
\begin{array}{cc}
A & \boxed{a} \\
B & \boxed{b} \\
C & \boxed{c}
\end{array}
\quad \Longrightarrow \quad
\begin{array}{c}
\boxed{b} \\
\boxed{c} \\
\boxed{-}
\end{array}
$$

$$
\textit{Low Priority Back Ptr} \quad \boxed{-} \quad \Longrightarrow \quad \boxed{a}
$$

Puts the contents of the A register into the low priority back pointer register. This instruction should not be used for manipulating the contents of the process queue, because no interlock mechanism is provided to prevent the processor accessing the queue while a user program is in the middle of modifying them. During booting, it is not in fact necessary to initialise the back pointers since the transputer can detect the special case of no active processes (front pointer = *MinInt*) and take appropriate action.

STLF   21 FC

Store Low Priority Front
Pointer

$$
\begin{array}{c}
A \\ B \\ C
\end{array}
\begin{array}{|c|}
\hline a \\ \hline b \\ \hline c \\ \hline
\end{array}
\quad \Longrightarrow \quad
\begin{array}{|c|}
\hline b \\ \hline c \\ \hline - \\ \hline
\end{array}
$$

$$
\textit{Low Priority Front Ptr} \quad
\begin{array}{|c|}
\hline - \\ \hline
\end{array}
\quad \Longrightarrow \quad
\begin{array}{|c|}
\hline a \\ \hline
\end{array}
$$

Puts the contents of the A register into the low priority front pointer register. This instruction should only be used for initialising the low priority process queue. It should not be used for manipulating the contents of the process queue, because no interlock mechanism is provided to prevent the processor accessing the queue while a user program is in the middle of modifying them.

Example

Initialise the low priority process queue. This must be done after a reset before any scheduling operations can be performed.

opcode	mnemonic	C	B	A
		c	b	a
	; initialise front pointer			
24 F2	MINT	b	a	80000000
21 FC	STLF	$-$	b	a

STNL n

En

Store Non-Local

```
A  | a |        | c |
B  | b |   ⟹    | - |
C  | c |        | - |

[a&n] | - |  ⟹  | b |
```

Stores a value at an address not in the local workspace (c.f. **LDNL**). The value in B is stored at an offset n from the address specified in the A register. The range of the offset may be extended through the use of the positive and negative prefix instructions.

Example

Store #8E7 in the third word of a table starting at location #3F0 (see also **LDNL** for an example of non-local variable access)

opcode	mnemonic	C	B	A	[#3F8]
		c	b	a	-
28 2E 47	LDC #8E7	b	a	8E7	-
23 2F 40	LDC #3F0	a	8E7	3F0	-
E2	STNL 2	-	-	a	8E7

STOPERR   25 F5

Stop On Error

IF *Error Flag* set THEN

$$
\begin{array}{ccc}
\text{A} & \boxed{a} & \\
\text{B} & \boxed{b} & \Longrightarrow \\
\text{C} & \boxed{c} &
\end{array}
\qquad
\begin{array}{c}
\boxed{-} \\
\boxed{-} \\
\boxed{-}
\end{array}
$$

$$
[w\&{-}1] \ \boxed{-} \quad \Longrightarrow \quad \boxed{i}
$$

Another active process is selected
ELSE

$$
\begin{array}{ccc}
\text{A} & \boxed{a} & \\
\text{B} & \boxed{b} & \Longrightarrow \\
\text{C} & \boxed{c} &
\end{array}
\qquad
\begin{array}{c}
\boxed{a} \\
\boxed{b} \\
\boxed{c}
\end{array}
$$

(Note: i is the address of the following instruction.)

If the error flag is set, the instruction pointer is stored at offset -1 in the local workspace and another process is selected from one of the queues. Otherwise execution continues normally. This instruction is equivalent to executing **Stop Process** if the error flag is set. Note that once the process is suspended, it will never be reactivated unless another process explicitly executes a **Run Process** instruction.

STOPP   21 F5

Stop Process

$$\begin{array}{cc} \begin{array}{cc} A & \boxed{a} \\ B & \boxed{b} \\ C & \boxed{c} \end{array} & \Longrightarrow & \begin{array}{c} \boxed{-} \\ \boxed{-} \\ \boxed{-} \end{array} \\[2em] [w\&{-}1] \; \boxed{-} & \Longrightarrow & \boxed{i} \end{array}$$

Another active process is selected

(Note: i is the address of the following instruction.)

The instruction pointer I is stored at offset -1 from the workspace pointer and the process is descheduled. Execution continues with another process selected from one of the queues. The instruction pointer is saved in the workspace to allow the process to be subsequently restarted by a RUNP instruction if required. Note that once the process is suspended, it will never be reactivated unless another process explicitly executes the Run Process instruction.

Example

A process executing at location #1A0 is stopped.

opcode	mnemonic	C	B	A	$[w\&{-}1]$	I
		c	b	a	–	1A0
21 F5	STOPP	–	–	–	1A2	*next process*

STTIMER   25 F4

Store Timer

$$
\begin{array}{cc}
\begin{array}{cc}
A & \boxed{a} \\
B & \boxed{b} \\
C & \boxed{c}
\end{array}
&
\Longrightarrow
&
\begin{array}{c}
\boxed{b} \\
\boxed{c} \\
\boxed{-}
\end{array}
\end{array}
$$

$$
\begin{array}{cc}
\begin{array}{cc}
\textit{Low priority Timer} & \boxed{-} \\
\textit{High priority Timer} & \boxed{-}
\end{array}
&
\Longrightarrow
&
\begin{array}{c}
\boxed{a} \\
\boxed{a}
\end{array}
\end{array}
$$

The contents of the A register is stored in both the low and high priority timer registers and the timers are started. This instruction is used for initialising the timers after a reset or analyse.

SUB

FC

Signed Subtraction

$$
\begin{array}{cc}
\text{A} & \boxed{a} \\
\text{B} & \boxed{b} \\
\text{C} & \boxed{c}
\end{array}
\quad \Longrightarrow \quad
\boxed{\begin{array}{c} b - a \\ c \\ - \end{array}}
$$

Error Flag set if arithmetic overflow occurs

Returns the result of the signed integer subtraction of the top two values on the stack. Overflow is checked for and the error flag is set if it occurs.

Example

Subtract #C02 from #AB0 and leave the result on the stack.

opcode	mnemonic	C	B	A
		c	*b*	*a*
2A 2B 40	LDC #AB0	*b*	*a*	AB0
2C 20 42	LDC #C02	*a*	AB0	C02
FC	SUB	–	*a*	FFFFFEAE

SUM   25 F2

Unsigned Addition

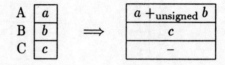

Returns the result of the unsigned addition of the top two values on the stack. Overflow is not checked for and the error flag is not modified.

Example

Add #C02 and #AB0 together.

opcode	mnemonic	C	B	A
		c	*b*	*a*
2A 2B 40	LDC #AB0	*b*	*a*	AB0
2C 20 42	LDC #C02	*a*	AB0	C02
25 F2	SUM	–	*a*	16B2

TALT

24 FE

Timer Alt Start

$$
\begin{array}{c}
\begin{array}{r}
\text{A} \\ \text{B} \\ \text{C}
\end{array}
\begin{array}{|c|}
\hline a \\ \hline b \\ \hline c \\ \hline
\end{array}
\implies
\begin{array}{|c|}
\hline a \\ \hline b \\ \hline c \\ \hline
\end{array}
\end{array}
$$

$$
\begin{array}{r}
[w\&{-}3] \\ [w\&{-}4]
\end{array}
\begin{array}{|c|}
\hline - \\ \hline - \\ \hline
\end{array}
\implies
\begin{array}{|c|}
\hline MinInt + 1 \\ \hline MinInt + 2 \\ \hline
\end{array}
$$

This instruction is designed for use in the implementation of the occam **ALT** construct. It should be used instead of **Alt Start** in situations where at least one of the **ALT** guards is waiting on a time. It performs the same function as **Alt Start**, but in addition, initialises location −4 to *MinInt* + 2 to indicate that no valid time has yet been stored. See **Alt Start** for more information.

Example

Since this instruction is really only meaningful when used along with other **ALT** instructions, a full example is not given; instead, we will show its effect in isolation. For a discussion of how the various ALT instructions interact, see page 43.

opcode	mnemonic	C	B	A	[w&−3]	[w&−4]
		c	b	a	−	−
24 FE	TALT	c	b	a	80000001	80000002

TALTWT   25 F1

Timer Alt Wait

$$
\begin{array}{ll}
\text{A} & \boxed{a} \\
\text{B} & \boxed{b} \\
\text{C} & \boxed{c}
\end{array}
\implies
\begin{array}{l}
\boxed{-} \\
\boxed{-} \\
\boxed{-}
\end{array}
$$

$$
w \;\boxed{-} \implies \boxed{-1}
$$

IF ($[w\&-3]$ = $MinInt+1$)
   OR ((($[w\&-4]$ = $MinInt+1$) AND
      ($[w\&-5]$ BEFORE *current time*))
THEN the next instruction is executed
ELSE The time to wait until, ie $[w\&-5]$, is put
        into timer queue, the process is descheduled and

$$
[w\&-3]\;\boxed{MinInt+1}\implies\boxed{MinInt+2}
$$

This instruction is designed for use in the implementation of the occam **ALT** construct. It should be used instead of **Alt Wait** in situations where at least one of the **ALT** guards is waiting on a time. It performs the same function as **Alt Wait**, but in addition, checks to see if a timer guard has fired, i.e. there exists a valid time ($[w\&-4]$ = $MinInt+1$) and that time is earlier than the current time. If no guards have fired the process is added to the timer queue. See **Alt Wait** for more information.

This instruction may take an arbitrary length of time to execute, since it may have to insert the **ALT** process at an arbitrary point in the timer queue. Thus, it has been made interruptable in order to improve interrupt latency for high priority processes.

Example

Since this instruction is really only meaningful when used along with other **ALT** instructions, a full example is not given; instead, we will show its effect in isolation. For a discussion of how the various ALT instructions interact, see page 43.

opcode	mnemonic	C	B	A	[w&–3]	[w]
		c	b	a	80000001	–
25 F1	**TALTWT**	–	–	–	80000001	–1
	process has been descheduled					

TESTERR   22 F9

Test Error False and Clear

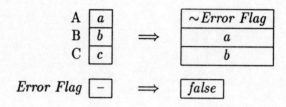

The TESTERR instruction loads *false* onto the stack if the error flag is set and *true* otherwise. The error flag is then cleared. This instruction's main use is during initialisation after a reset or analyse. It can also be used for implementing error recovery schemes that do not use the transputer's halt-on-error mode. The error flag is then left in the clear state to facilitate the checking of errors over the next piece of code.

Example

Perform a signed subtraction and then test for overflow.

opcode	mnemonic	C	B	A	Error Flag
		c	*b*	*a*	*false*
24 F2	MINT	*b*	*a*	80000000	*false*
41	LDC 1	*a*	80000000	1	*false*
FC	SUB	–	*a*	7FFFFFFF	*true*
22 F9	TESTERR	*a*	7FFFFFFF	0	*false*
Ax	CJ error			*jump executed*	

TESTHALTERR 25 F9

Test Halt-On-Error Flag

A	a		*Halt-On-Error Flag*	
B	b	$\Longrightarrow$	a	
C	c		b	

This instruction tests the state of the halt-on-error flag, and puts *true* (1) on the stack if set, *false* (0) otherwise.

The halt-on-error flag governs the action of the processor when the error flag becomes set. If the halt-on-error flag is set, the processor will halt when the error flag becomes set. If the halt-on-error flag is clear, the processor will continue with the next instruction when the error flag becomes set.

Example

If the halt-on-error flag is set then:

opcode	mnemonic	C	B	A
		c	b	a
25 F9	TESTHALTERR	b	a	1

TESTPRANAL   22 FA

Test Processor Analysing

$$
\begin{array}{cc}
\text{A} & \boxed{a} \\
\text{B} & \boxed{b} \\
\text{C} & \boxed{c}
\end{array}
\quad \Longrightarrow \quad
\begin{array}{|c|}
\hline
\textit{Analyse Flag} \\
\hline
a \\
\hline
b \\
\hline
\end{array}
$$

The **TESTPRANAL** instruction allows the executing process to determine whether or not the processor was last reset with the analyse signal asserted. If this is the case, then *true* (1) is pushed onto the evaluation stack, otherwise *false* (0) is stored. This instruction is intended for use in the bootstrap routine to allow the selection of either the regular bootstrap process or special diagnostic process.

TIN

22 FB

Timer Input

Let

a = the time at which the process is to be rescheduled.

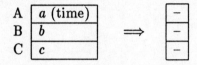

Note: this instruction may cause the process to be descheduled.

Wait until a specified time. If the specified time is in the past, the instruction has no effect. If the specified time is in the future, the process is suspended until that time. The transputer represents time by a single word whose value is incremented at regular intervals (the interval depends on the process priority and the processor speed). When the time value reaches the most positive integer its value wraps round to the most negative integer. When comparing a specified time with the current time, current times between a and $a +_{\text{unsigned}} MinInt$ are considered to be in the future and all the other values of the specified time are considered to be in the past.

This instruction may take an arbitrary length of time to execute, since it may have to insert the process at an arbitrary point in the timer queue. Thus, it has been made interruptable in order to improve interrupt latency for high priority processes.

Example

Suspend the current process until #1000 time units after the current time.

opcode	mnemonic	C	B	A
		c	*b*	*a*
21 20 20				
40	LDC #1000	*b*	*a*	1000
22 F2	LDTIMER	*a*	1000	73F87AC1
25 F2	SUM	–	*a*	73F88AC1
22 FB	TIN	–	–	–

UNPACKSN 26 F3

Unpack Single Length
Floating Point Number

Let

$a = $ a single-length floating-point number;

$$type = \begin{cases} 0 & \text{if } a \text{ is zero} \\ 1 & \text{if } a \text{ is normalised} \\ 2 & \text{if } a \text{ is infinity} \\ 3 & \text{if } a \text{ is Not-A-Number} \end{cases}$$

THEN

A	a
B	b
C	c

$\Longrightarrow$

fraction field of a
exponent field of a
$4b + type$

Note: this instruction is specific to the T414.

This instruction unpacks the various fields of a floating-point number. It is intended for use in implementing floating point software packages for the T414.

WCNT   23 FF

Word Count

Let

k = number of byte select bits in a word (2 for the T414).

THEN

$$
\begin{array}{cc}
A & \boxed{a} \\
B & \boxed{b} \\
C & \boxed{c}
\end{array}
\implies
\begin{array}{|c|}
\hline
a \gg k \\
\hline
a \wedge (2^k - 1) \\
\hline
b \\
\hline
\end{array}
$$

This instruction converts a memory pointer (contained in A) into a word address (returned in A) and a byte index into the word (returned in B).

Example

Find the word address and byte offset of the word at offset 3 in the local workspace. We assume that the local workspace is at location #F00.

opcode	mnemonic	C	B	A
		c	b	a
13	LDLP 3	b	a	F0C
23 FF	WCNT	a	0	3C3

WSUB

FA

Word Subscript

$$
\begin{array}{c}
A \; \boxed{a} \\
B \; \boxed{b} \\
C \; \boxed{c}
\end{array}
\implies
\begin{array}{c}
\boxed{a\&b} \\
\boxed{c} \\
\boxed{-}
\end{array}
$$

Evaluates the address of a word in a word array. The base address of the array is in the A register and the word offset from this base is in the B register. Its use for accessing word arrays (instead of using SUM) ensures the word length independence of the code. Note that this instruction is undefined if the byte selector bits of A are non-zero.

Example

Find the address of the 2nd word in an array starting at offset 3 in the local workspace. We assume that the local workspace is at location #F00.

opcode	mnemonic	C	B	A
		c	b	a
41	LDC 1	b	a	1
13	LDLP 3	a	1	F0C
F2	WSUB	–	a	F10

XDBLE   21 FD

Extend to Double

IF $a < 0$ THEN

$$
\begin{array}{c}
A \\
B \\
C
\end{array}
\begin{array}{|c|}
\hline a \\
\hline b \\
\hline c \\
\hline
\end{array}
\quad \Longrightarrow \quad
\begin{array}{|c|}
\hline a \\
\hline -1 \\
\hline b \\
\hline
\end{array}
$$

ELSE

$$
\begin{array}{c}
A \\
B \\
C
\end{array}
\begin{array}{|c|}
\hline a \\
\hline b \\
\hline c \\
\hline
\end{array}
\quad \Longrightarrow \quad
\begin{array}{|c|}
\hline a \\
\hline 0 \\
\hline b \\
\hline
\end{array}
$$

Sign extends the single length value in A into a double length value in the register pair BA (low order word in A). The value that B takes depends on the state of the top bit of the A register. If this bit is set, B takes the value -1, if clear, B takes the value 0.

Example

Convert *MinInt* into a 64-bit value.

opcode	mnemonic	C	B	A
		c	*b*	*a*
24 F2	MINT	*b*	*a*	80000000
F2	WSUB	*a*	FFFFFFFF	80000000

XOR   23 F3

Bitwise Exclusive-OR

$$
\begin{array}{cc}
\text{A} & \boxed{a} \\
\text{B} & \boxed{b} \\
\text{C} & \boxed{c}
\end{array}
\quad\Longrightarrow\quad
\begin{array}{c}
\boxed{a \oplus b} \\
\boxed{c} \\
\boxed{-}
\end{array}
$$

Performs a bitwise exclusive-OR between the top two operands on the stack.

Example

Perform an exclusive-OR between #C2 and #AB.

opcode	mnemonic	C	B	A
		c	b	a
2C 42	LDC #C2	b	a	C2
2A 4B	LDC #AB	a	C2	AB
23 F3	XOR	−	a	69

XWORD   23 FA

Extend to Word

Let

a = subrange mask, $= 2^{k-1}$ where k is the number of
  bits in the subrange,
b = value to be extended to word length.

IF $b \geq_{\text{unsigned}} a$ THEN

A	a		$b - 2a$
B	b	$\Longrightarrow$	c
C	c		–

ELSE

A	a		b
B	b	$\Longrightarrow$	c
C	c		–

Sign extends a subword length integer to word length. Register B
contains the subrange value to be extended and A contains a value that
defines the bit length of the subrange. This value should have the sign bit
of the subrange set and all the other bits reset; that is, the most negative
representable number of the subrange. The effect of the instruction (if
the input value is within the specified subrange) is to copy the subrange
sign bit into all the bits above it in the word. The instruction definition
$b \geq_{\text{unsigned}} a$ may seem a bit strange at first, but all it is really saying, is
that if the value b, treated as a 32-bit unsigned integer, is greater than or
equal to a, then the partword value represented by b must be negative.
Subtracting $2a$ from b just has the effect of changing the top bits in the
word from zeros to ones.

Example

Load the 3rd entry of a packed array of 4-bit subrange values and convert it to word length. The array starts at offset 0 in the local workspace.

opcode	mnemonic	C	B	A
		c	*b*	*a*
	; *load the word that contains the third entry*			
70	LDL 0	*b*	*a*	EF3DB92C
	; *isolate the required four bit field*			
2F 20 40	LDC #F00	*a*	EF3DB92C	00000F00
24 F6	AND	–	*a*	00000900
	; *shift down to bottom four bits*			
48	LDC 8	*a*	00000900	8
24 F0	SHR	–	*a*	00000009
	; *extend to word length*			
48	LDC 8	*a*	00000009	8
23 FA	XWORD	–	*a*	FFFFFFF9

Appendix A

Transputer Opcodes

	xn	Fx	21 Fx	22 Fx	23 Fx
0	J n	REV	SETERR	RET	DISS
1	LDLP n	LB		LEND	LMUL
2	PFIX n	BSUB	RESETCH	LDTIMER	NOT
3	LDNL n	ENDP	CSUB0		XOR
4	LDC n	DIFF			BCNT
5	LDNLP n	ADD	STOPP		LSHR
6	NFIX n	GCALL	LADD		LSHL
7	LDL n	IN	STLB		LSUM
8	ADC n	PROD	STHF		LSUB
9	CALL n	GT	NORM	TESTERR	RUNP
A	CJ n	WSUB	LDIV	TESTPRANAL	XWORD
B	AJW n	OUT	LDPI	TIN	SB
C	EQC n	SUB	STLF	DIV	GAJW
D	STL n	STARTP	XDBLE		SAVEL
E	STNL n	OUTBYTE	LDPRI	DIST	SAVEH
F	OPR n	OUTWORD	REM	DISC	WCNT

	24 Fx	25 Fx	26 Fx	27 Fx	
0	SHR	STHB			
1	SHL	TALTWT		LDINF	
2	MINT	SUM		FMUL	
3	ALT	MUL	UNPACKSN	CFLERR	
4	ALTWT	STTIMER			
5	ALTEND	STOPERR			
6	AND	CWORD			
7	ENBT	CLRHALTERR			
8	ENBC	SETHALTERR			
9	ENBS	TESTHALTERR			
A	MOVE				
B	OR				
C	CSNGL		POSTNORMSN		
D	CCNT1		ROUNDSN		
E	TALT				
F	LDIFF				

Appendix B

Symbols

These are the symbols used for the formal definitions of the instruction set in the reference section.

symbol	meaning
A	top element of evaluation stack
B	middle element of evaluation stack
C	bottom element of evaluation stack
W	workspace pointer
I	instruction pointer
a, b, c, w, i	initial contents the above registers
n	the operand of the instruction
&	word indexing ($a \& i = a + 2^k i$ for some k)
$\&_{\text{byte}}$	byte indexing ($a \&_{\text{byte}} i \simeq a + i$)
[ ]	word contents of
$[\ ]_{\text{byte}}$	byte contents of
$\wedge$	bitwise AND
$\vee$	bitwise OR
$\oplus$	bitwise exclusive-OR
$\ll$	shift left x places
$\gg$	shift right x places
$MinInt$	minimum integer $= 2^{\text{wordlength}-1}$
–	a value that is undefined or unimportant

Appendix C

Workspace Usage

This table shows what use the scheduling hardware makes of various words below the workspace of a process.

Offset	Value held	Under what conditions
0	*data to transfer*	during OUTBYTE or OUTWORD execution
	jump offset	during ALT disabling
−1	*instruction pointer*	whenever a process is descheduled
−2	*ptr to next process*	the process is descheduled but ready
	in active queue	to proceed
−3	*MinInt*+1	process is an ALT, no guards fired yet
	MinInt+2	process descheduled after ALTWT
	MinInt+3	process is an ALT, and a guard has fired
	valid address	process is descheduled, awaiting channel communication
−4	*MinInt*+1	indicates a valid time at offset −5 during a timer ALT
	MinInt+2	indicates no valid time at offset −5
−5	*a time*	the time to wait until during a timer ALT

Appendix D

Instruction Cross-references

Bibliography

[1] *occam 2 Reference Manual*, (1988) Prentice Hall International, UK.

[2] Brookes G. R. and Stewart A. J. (1989) *Introduction to occam 2 on the Transputer*, Macmillan, London.

[3] *Transputer Development System*, (1988) Prentice Hall International, UK.

[4] *Transputer Instruction Set: A Compiler Writer's Guide*, (1988) Prentice Hall International, UK.

[5] Shephard R. (1987) *Extraordinary Use of Transputer Links.* INMOS Technical Note 1.

Index